Finding a Better Way

Exploring old and new ideas
across country, workplace,
community and family

finding a better way

DAVID BANGER
MICHELLE STEVENSON

db davidbanger

Copyright © David Banger and Michelle Stevenson 2021

All models copyright © David Banger 2021

First published in 2021 in Melbourne

Typeset and cover design by BookPOD

ISBN: 978-0-6486968-2-7 (pbk) 978-0-6486968-3-4 (e-book)

NATIONAL LIBRARY OF AUSTRALIA

A catalogue record for this book is available from the National Library of Australia

Epigraph

'When you grow up, you tend to get told that the world is the way it is and your [job] is just to live your life inside the world, try not to bash into the walls too much, try to have a nice family life, have fun, save a little money.

'That's a very limited life. Life can be much broader, once you discover one simple fact, and that is everything around you that you call life was made up by people that were no smarter than you. And you can change it, you can influence it, you can build your own things that other people can use. Once you learn that, you'll never be the same again.

'The minute that you understand that you can poke life and actually something will, you know if you push in, something will pop out the other side, that you can change it, you can mould it. That's maybe the most important thing. It's to shake off this erroneous notion that life is there and you're just gonna live in it, versus embrace it, change it, improve it, make your mark upon it.

'I think that's very important and however you learn that, once you learn it, you'll want to change life and make it better, cause it's kind of messed up, in a lot of ways. Once you learn that, you'll never be the same again.'

– Steve Jobs

CONTENTS

The Potential of Systems Thinking

'The world is made of circles and we think in straight lines.'

– Peter Senge

David: It was a coolish yet very sunning morning at Warwick Business School, in Coventry in the United Kingdom, in 2002. My employer was running the third cohort of its internal university program and there were about thirty of us in attendance. The company was determined to create a core group of internal influencers (this was the early 2000s – long before the term was used to refer to those who are paid for their social media activity) to build on the solid foundations of the past, but with a focus on creating a company for this century.

We were told from the outset that we were not the most senior employees of the organisation. However, we were in some ways the most important due to the impact we each could have. We were encouraged to listen, think, quietly reflect on and discuss what triggered our interest during the week-long program. We were to become systems thinkers.

Peter Senge is an MIT professor who is a leading expert in systems thinking. Systems thinking focuses on how an individual part (either natural or human-made) interacts with the other parts of the system it exists within.

The world is 'interconnected' and 'interdependent', which means an action somewhere has influence elsewhere. At the time of writing this sentence, my family is in isolation at our home in Melbourne due to COVID-19, which has sadly spread across the world. This pandemic is an example of how connected we are and how dependent we are on other people's actions.

Of course, not everything is this direct and dramatic. There are quiet global shifts occurring over time that may not appear to be connected, as they happen within a single country. Eventually, however, they amount to an outcome that impacts all of us. An event or action within one country influences the outcome for other countries.

In our recent human history, technology has exacerbated this. We are now connected to every corner of the world. Technology continues to evolve rapidly and is likely to have unexpected impacts in the future. For instance, people are now connected with others who have similar interests, regardless of where they may be in the world. Many of us are members of global online communities.

This notion of interconnectedness is not a new phenomenon. In fact, the Industrial Age, which took place in the 18th and 19th centuries, created a whole new world of interconnectedness. Where something was created was not necessarily where it would be used. This meant that many hands would touch something before it arrived at its destination. Nowadays, this is considered the norm across multiple facets of daily life; the products we purchase and the foods we consume are from everywhere. Similarly, a decision we make can or will affect people in another part of the world. In this way, we are living in each other's backyards – for better or worse.

Senge offers the example of the canals in Northern India that are now dry, but they never used to be. The source of these river systems originates in the Himalayas. As the glaciers have contracted, the spring melt has grown increasingly smaller, which means all these river systems are at the lowest levels they have ever been. The glaciers are contracting due to global warming – the consequence of electricity use across the world. According to Senge, a contributing factor to India's dry rivers is the charging of our phones every night, which requires the burning of coal for electricity.

To understand a system, you need to take a step back to understand the truth, then step back further. You must constantly step back to really understand what is going on.

In 2015, Senge was working with Google, and together they estimated that twenty per cent of the world's energy is spent powering our gadgets. This is more than we use to power our homes and it is growing rapidly. It is the wealthy and middle class who are driving the use of this power, and who are having a profound impact on the poor. There are 150 million dehydrated people in Northern India, Pakistan and Afghanistan. Access to water is one of the biggest problems in the world, and it continues to worsen. A little fewer than a billion people have access to reliable drinking water.

Our interconnectedness has increased, but Senge believes our ability to understand that has declined. That is why Michelle and I have dedicated the preface of our book to systems thinking.

As you read on, we encourage you to step back from the details to see the bigger picture and explore what is influencing the situation at hand. Here are some questions to keep in mind:

- When stepping back, you need to be mindful of the factors that may influence your perspective. How might your beliefs and values inform the way you see a situation?
- How are you contributing to and influencing a situation?
- Can you consider broader and more diverse perspectives to see a situation in a different way?
- Who is not being acknowledged and heard, and how might they see the situation?
- When considering other perspectives, how might your assumptions be tested?

This line of questioning is incredibly important, as it serves to better inform your decisions and actions. Here are some additional questions to consider:

- If you were to take action in a particular situation, what might happen?
- Can you draw a model or a picture, or use a metaphor, to help reveal new insights? (I like both, as they help make sense of a complex situation.)

As you read this book, we encourage you to look for connections and relationships between parts of a complex situation. Is there an emerging or recurring pattern? Also, be sure to reflect on what you're reading. Ask yourself: What have I learned about a particular system and how can I apply this knowledge going forward? We have reflections included at the end of every chapter, with some questions. This is not exhaustive and you may have some different thoughts. These are encouraged!

My children are growing up with an awareness of the world. Senge says that children are very aware, but they are also pessimistic about the future of the planet. However, he believes that many can become very effective systems thinkers because of their innate awareness. His work has found that adults are less connected with the living system of the world than ever before, and it continues to deteriorate. At the same time, our interconnectedness is increasing. The world is interconnected more than ever before, across countries, workplaces, communities and families.

Our problem now is not that we don't understand inter-connectedness, as we are deeply interconnected. Our problem is that we are not stepping back. That is, stepping back to better understand how we live – and how we might improve. We have an opportunity to encourage our children to do just that.

In order to do that, it's important to understand the difference between human systems and technology. Humans do not simply take in sensory data, like a machine does, and record it. A machine sees something as it is. As humans, we do not perceive the world we see. Rather, we see the world we perceive, and our perception is influenced by our history. This is the Santiago theory of cognition, developed by Chilean biologist turned philosopher Humberto Maturana.

Often, our intent can be good and honourable, but it can create conflict, nonetheless. For example, you may say something that causes offence to someone else. That was not your intention, but it was how the other person interpreted your words, based on their own personal history and reality. As interconnectedness increases, situations become more complicated, as we have many human systems interacting with different realities. This is why it was important for me not to write this book alone; it is a better book with Michelle's contribution, as her thoughts offer a different reality.

We must stress that we do not want to tell you how to think, nor seek your compliance regarding our thoughts. When another human being tells another, 'This is what is really going on here,' they are demanding obedience. Neither Michelle nor I want that. We simply want to encourage you to think about things more deeply, and then make up your own mind – and potentially even take thoughtful action after stepping back.

We want to raise your awareness of human relationships in the world. Many personal conflicts are simply due to people's different realities. When people are grounded and curious, there is humility. Only then will people truly listen to one another. I am more curious now than ever before. My life experiences across countries and communities continue to raise my interest in our interconnectedness.

Here are some final questions to keep in mind and reflect on as you read this book:

- How have the experiences in your life shaped your perception of the world?
- Have those experiences led to bias? Can you identify any of those biases as you are reading?

A final suggestion: You do not need to read this book sequentially; you can jump to sections that interest you. The sections we have included are not an exhaustive synopsis of all the related systems. They are what we determined to be of interest (here's hoping they are!). They are the tip of the iceberg and we have included some personal stories throughout the book. These help to break the book up a little and may offer some insights into why we chose a certain piece of research.

As I said earlier, there is also a reflection at the end of each chapter. These are designed to wrap up our thoughts in a succinct way, and we encourage you to consider your own thoughts before moving on to another section.

Shaking the Pillars

'I don't believe you have to be better than everybody else. I believe you have to be better than you ever thought you could be.'

– Ken Venturi

Michelle: As people who have been brought up in Western societies, many of us believe that we are 'better'. Not just better than those who are different to us, but better than each other too.

Better than people older or younger than us.

Better than our co-worker, who is always late to meetings.

Better than our neighbour, whose lawn is never mowed.

Better than the single mum trying to juggle it all.

Better than the garbage truck guy.

Better *how*, exactly?

By potentially knowing more, doing more, earning more, consuming more...the list could be endless.

But are these the things we should measure ourselves against? Our obsession with being 'better' than those around us has created an unhealthy balance in our world, a 'rat race', whereby we compromise our true beliefs and values to make 'progress'. We may ignore what we intuitively know, simply because we do not have the time to think about it more deeply (or, at least, we don't think we have the time).

We hope this book prompts you to think about things more deeply. Because we feel there is a different way to be better.

We are asking you, dear reader, to join us as we consider an alternate path. To do this, we must first understand what has led us to this point, and how things could be different – collectively and individually. To help us frame our thoughts (and yours), we have divided the book into four parts:

- **Part 1: Country** (chapters one and two)
- **Part 2: Workplace** (chapters three and four)
- **Part 3: Community** (chapters five and six)
- **Part 4: Family** (chapters seven and eight)

We believe these are the four core pillars that make up most people's lives. Each part of the book contains two chapters – one that looks at each of these pillars from a global perspective, and one from the perspective of our current home here in Australia.

As David said in the preface, you do not need to read the book in sequential order, or even in its entirety. We have written it in such a way that you can jump between chapters and subtopics based on what interests you. (Think of it as a sort of 'choose your own adventure' book!) In each chapter, you will find research, commentary and personal stories from both of us. Our hope is that you will reflect on the makeup of these pillars as they apply to you, and perhaps shake them up a bit.

Two voices are better than one

'If two people were exactly alike, one of them would be unnecessary.'

– Larry Dixon

Michelle: This book has two authors – David and myself. We decided to co-write the book within an hour of meeting each other face to face, and we believe our partnership gives the book a special point of difference. Allow me to introduce myself properly (David will introduce himself in the next section).

My name is Michelle Stevenson. I am a professional editor and writer, with a special interest in book editing. I began my career in journalism before segueing into editing, ultimately becoming senior editor at a major publishing company, where I continue to work. I also do a lot of freelance editing, most notably for a company called Grammar Factory, which helps entrepreneurs write and publish books.

Given the nature of my work, I have been asked many times throughout my career whether I might write a book myself. As is all too common among women my age, I routinely downplayed the idea, namely due to self-doubt. Could *I* really write a book? Who would want to read it?

That was my stance for several years. Until I met David.

When I marched into our impromptu meeting on February 24, 2020, it was not my intention to sell myself as a co-author for the new book he was writing. But after hearing his thoughts about what the book would entail, I knew I had to be involved. Not only because it was an opportunity that may never present itself again – but because I truly believed I could offer value to the book.

David was born in the seventies. He is a Generation X male. I was born in 1987. I am a Generation Y female. An unlikely pair, but that is exactly why we believe it is so powerful. This book is not inherently 'male' or 'female', or written to favour one generation over another. It is a dialogue of sorts, offering, at times, different viewpoints on some of the biggest challenges facing Western societies today.

Despite our differences, David and I also share some similarities. I grew up in Perth, Western Australia; David spent part of his boyhood there. We've both lived and worked overseas – he in London, and me in Canada and also Thailand.

And while we're both exceptionally privileged to lead our lives as white, educated people, we've both known adversity. David lost his mother at the age of six. He never completed high school and returned to night school in his mid-twenties to complete his studies. Meanwhile, I have watched both my father and stepfather suffer from Parkinson's disease. And in 2019, my husband (aged just thirty-one at the time) suffered a stroke, leaving him with a speech impairment. For me, this book has formed a big part of the healing process.

I am not telling you these things to garner sympathy. Rather, in sharing some of the details of our respective journeys, I hope to highlight the complexities of modern life. I encourage you to reflect on your own life experiences as you read this book. Our experiences shape who we are, and can influence the path we take, but we still have the power to turn in a new direction – if only by changing our mindset.

Restlessness leads to evolution

*'Restlessness is discontent and discontent
is the first necessity of progress.
Show me a thoroughly satisfied man
and I will show you a failure.'*

– Thomas Edison

David: My name is David Banger. I am a son, father, brother, cousin and friend. I am an author, adjunct professor, former CIO and digital executive, and I am now a CXO advisor in my own business. I have been employed across many industries, including construction and engineering, professional services, technology, management consulting and financial services.

My skill is offering unique and sharp insights that enable organisations and their people to progress and, ultimately, realise their full potential. I now work with CXOs and their teams who are committed to changing. I am a deep thinker. In my private time, I reflect on things a lot – this is always evident within my client work and within this book. These insights lead me to drive effective change for my clients.

In 2018, I founded CHANGE lead | Practical Digital® to bring my experience to organisations that value it. The business is more of a specialist practice rather than a large enterprise. I work closely with my clients on complex problems, and I enjoy it immensely, particularly when my insights lead to actions that break my clients out of a cycle.

My career began in an unorthodox way, as I left high school at sixteen without completing my high school certificate. I returned to formal education in my twenties, gaining under-

and postgraduate (MBA) qualifications (thank you, Swinburne University).

This book has been within me for over a decade, but I was not ready to write it until 2020. My experience and professional connections, combined with the right timing, have made it possible. In this regard, I am grateful for 2020 and the Melbourne lockdown. My first book, *Digital Is Everyone's Business*, was about my career experiences, in the hope of sharing my professional learnings and wisdom from others. This book is about some broader observations, passions, learnings from many people and a little insight I have gained along the way.

Michelle and I explore some global trends, at times with a focus on Australia, where we both live. Some of the topics we explore include the implications of globalisation, how communities now exist and the family of this century. There is an extensive amount of research included in the book, much of it completed by Michelle after our first meeting. Any additional research I did was inspired by her initial extraordinary effort.

Michelle is tenacious in her work. Her first parcel of research consisted of over 100 reports and articles, totalling more than 65,000 words, with multiple links to other sources. These research topics were based on our shared thinking, and were the initial platform for our writing. The book weaves them together, beginning at the global macro level, with some gender-based threads throughout the book, and finally concluding within the home.

There are times when Michelle and I differ; we expect your viewpoint will differ again and we welcome this. Differences are a strength, for democracy and innovation. In caring about something, change can be achieved. It is how we move forward. Sometimes, we move forward without much thought. We hope this book inspires you to keep moving forward, but perhaps in a more considered way.

We both care deeply about what we have included in the book, and we think others need to be aware of these things, encouraged to consider what change they would like to see happen and how they could play a role within that change. This could be a growing awareness, a conversation or possibly some sort of action. We do not have all the answers. We share many insights, some of which will raise further questions rather than provide absolute clarity. We want you, the reader, to pause on a page, stop and think.

As I mentioned earlier, I think a lot. My thinking makes me restless – maybe I think too much. However, this restlessness has led to the creation of this book. Restlessness means not settling, not spectating, always learning and continually evolving. It also means caring for things, big and small, and we hope you care for some of these things too.

Thank you for taking the time to read this book. We sincerely hope you can take something from it. Please share it, talk about it and feel free to connect with us about it.

PART 1

COUNTRY

CHAPTER 1

Perceptions and Politics

'We are what we think. All that we are arises with our thoughts. With our thoughts, we make the world.'

– Buddha

Michelle: In this first chapter, we focus on the power of perception, particularly in the context of national pride, patriotism and politics. David explores the dark art of political campaigning, which is changing the way political campaigns are run (and won). He also discusses the idea of desperate men and the rise of 'risky' voting. Later, I offer a different perspective on this, suggesting other contributing factors at play.

National pride and patriotism

'He loves his country best who strives to make it best.'

– Robert G. Ingersoll

David: My family and I lived in London from 2001 to 2010, and I loved it. Londoners are proud people and I considered myself one of them; two of our three children were born there. We all benefited from living in the world's 'greatest capital city'. It grew our thinking, how we saw the world, our understanding of others, and what we thought was possible.

The building my family lived in was in Maida Vale, known as Little Venice due to the canals that we loved walking along. It is a beautiful spot in central London, which had an eclectic mix of people, all of whom shared the common spaces in harmony. At the time, I was working at Microsoft, which also embodied the spirit of diversity. As a member of the international technology team, I experienced the richness of the world virtually from our apartment, through video conferences with my colleagues from every corner of the world.

I am Australian by birth and a British citizen through my ancestry. My grandfather was English. He was born in Shanklin on the Isle of Wight and immigrated to Australia between world wars. The process of my wife and I becoming British citizens involved us living in the United Kingdom for four years to obtain permanent residency and an additional year to obtain citizenship. We were proud to become British citizens. So, when it was time to leave London and return to Melbourne for our children's schooling, it was one of the most difficult experiences of my adult life. My wife, Nicole, felt the same, particularly as we had spent half our adult life in London.

Both my nationalities are important to me, although I potentially take my adopted British citizenship slightly more seriously. When we were living in London, I registered with the Australian government as a non-resident and did not participate in voting. Yet, now, as a non-resident of the UK, I register every year with the City of Westminster so I can vote in every election. When my two daughters turn eighteen, they will be able to vote in these elections, as we have remained registered. Voting in the UK is not compulsory, whereas in Australia you are fined for not voting. Somehow, I feel my vote counts more in a country where it is not compulsory. This is silly, of course, as all votes count, but that is how I feel.

The voting experience is different in London. On a voting day in Australia, everyone is out and about. It is an event in the sense that there are cake stalls and sausage sizzles at your local primary school, which is where you vote. In the UK, my perception is that people are not as aware, as it is not an 'event' as such. Maybe this is why I think my vote counts more. In his TED Talk on perception, neuroscientist Beau Lotto explains that all new perceptions begin with a single question: Why? As voting is not compulsory in the UK, this is probably some of my 'why' to commit to it. Compare this to voting in Australia, where no one has to consider their 'why' since they have to vote anyway.

Also, there is a strong consciousness within me about respecting those who sacrificed their lives for the freedom of others. As Australians, we come together on April 25 to remember the dawn landing in Turkey for a battle we lost. My wife and I have visited Anzac Cove in Gallipoli, Turkey, where the Australian identity of mateship and courage was forged so strongly.

I have stood in these trenches and do not really want to imagine how terrifying it was for the soldiers who fought and died in them. I would not want my children to live through any conflict – and certainly nothing like the two world wars that devastated the world in the first half of the 20th century. Again, this is an experience that has informed my belief system and, therefore, my perceptions – particularly about national pride and patriotism.

In the next section, I discuss in more detail the topic of voting, which is being influenced by new, increasingly deviant systems and my vulnerable male peer group.

The dark art of political campaigning

'There's a dark side to everything.'

– Prince

David: Across the world, there has been a *shift* in political parties, from a traditional, class-based distinction to a distinction based on cultural attitudes and education. Traditional political parties have found it difficult to position themselves in this new dimension.

Why?

Research indicates traditional voters are reacting to an erosion of their value system in society. In the past, these voters' interests were the welfare state and trade unions. Both have been eroded, as political parties have implemented platforms in relation to immigration and civil rights. Some say that shift has fuelled the traditional voters' frustration as traditional, democratic rights are removed, with elected political parties implementing new platforms.

As we are all living longer, many voters have developed a longing for the past – either old political policies or, more broadly, the way a country once was. Campaigning has evolved to target voters based on their perceptions. For example, if a voter yearns for the past, they will be targeted in this way. Previously, campaigns would be balanced across a country by the respective parties. In other words, there would be a consistent message or tone from a party.

When and how did this change?

In the late 1990s, American political advertising operative Ian Gould finally had a political candidate who was so far behind in the polls that he agreed to spend $100,000 on banner ads on *The*

New York Times' homepage. These initial ads targeted specific audiences with tailored messages and then tracked their reaction. The tailored messages had a positive impact. Although Gould's candidate did not win, he captured more votes than expected.

In a *Slate* column published in 1999, then publisher Cyrus Krohn wrote, '*Come November 2000, I expect the question will no longer be whether Web-based political advertising works, but whether it works too well.*'

This started a new system, or cycle.

I am interested in cycles as I seek to change cycles in my professional work. I am often engaged by clients to assist with their business – specifically, their technical or digital strategy – and almost always end up working with people and the systems (systems thinking) within. Often, these cycles are not seen by people until I call them out. I am doing the same in this book, focusing here on the topic of political campaigning. I am not a political campaign analyst; others have researched this extensively and here is some of their research.

Not surprisingly, political campaigning now focuses on microtargeting voters. Microtargeting relies on transmitting a tailored message to a subgroup of the electorate based on unique information about that subgroup. This is done via direct mail, phone calls, home visits, television, radio, web advertising, email and text messaging.

In 2008, the year Barack Obama ran for office (and won), presidential candidates spent just $22.5 million on online political ads, according to an analysis by Borrell Associates. In 2016, campaigns spent a whopping $1.4 billion on digital ads. In 2020, the total cost of election campaigning hit $14 billion (as of November 2020).

According to *The Guardian*, Brad Parscale – who was the digital media director for Donald Trump's 2016 presidential campaign – ran up to 60,000 variations of Facebook ads *each day* during the campaign. Facebook banned political advertising after the 2020 election and extended the moratorium into November after polls closed in October.

Why?

Because social media political campaigning was so effective, this was Facebook's ongoing effort to protect the election. To help stop the spread of misinformation.

How has political campaigning become so effective?

Campaigns now include one message for one set of voters and another, completely different message for another set of voters. This is known as dark advertising. Cambridge Analytica is a now-defunct British political consulting firm, which gained notoriety after a major data breach in early 2018. The Facebook–Cambridge Analytica data breach saw millions of Facebook users' personal data harvested without consent by Cambridge Analytica. The data was predominantly used for political advertising.

Cambridge Analytica played a major role in various campaigns, including the 'Leave' campaign for Britain's European Union membership referendum (more commonly known as Brexit), and later became a key figure in digital operations during Trump's 2016 election campaign. In both cases, Cambridge Analytica's data analytics team was able to identify millions of voters based on their psychological weaknesses. As whistle blower Christopher Wylie told *The Observer*, '*We exploited Facebook to harvest millions of people's profiles. And built models to exploit what we knew about them and target their inner demons.*'

Exploiting people's 'inner demons' meant creating hundreds of political ads, memes and emails – many of which were misleading or in some cases untrue – that furthered the pro-Brexit and Trump campaigns.

According to a 2017 article by NBC News, an estimated 126 million Americans received Russian-backed content (fake news) in their Facebook news feeds during the 2016 election. The article states, '*Underscoring how widely content on the social media platform can spread, Facebook says in the testimony that while some 29 million Americans directly received material from 80,000 posts by 120 fake Russian-backed pages in their own news feeds, those posts were "shared, liked and followed by people on Facebook, and, as a result, three times more people may have been exposed to a story that originated from the Russian operation."*'

Fake news generated on social media is a serious issue. According to the UK Office of Communications (Ofcom), fewer than forty per cent of Britons trust news they read on social media. Meanwhile, half of all Americans view fake news as a bigger threat than terrorism, illegal immigration, violent crime or racism. The US is in the process of addressing some of the issue with a bipartisan bill known as the Honest Ads Act. The Brennan Center for Justice, a nonpartisan law and policy institute, said the proposed law would modernise campaign finance laws to account for online political advertising. The website states:

> '*The proposed legislation addresses a loophole in existing campaign finance laws, which regulate TV and radio ads but not internet ads. This loophole has allowed foreign entities to purchase online ads that mention political candidates. The Honest Ads Act would help close that loophole by subjecting internet ads to the same rules as TV and radio ads. It would also increase overall transparency by allowing the public to see who bought an online political ad, no matter who it was.*'

Desperate men and the rise of 'risky' voting

*'There are no desperate situations,
there are only desperate people.'*

– Heinz Guderian

David: The proliferation of information is contributing to the *cycle* mentioned earlier. It takes more information to believe something that you do not want to believe, so people are more willing to share social media content if it supports their beliefs. Remember that before sharing something in the future!

Last year, I 'unfriended' someone whom I have known and cared about for over twenty years. Throughout my life, I have befriended and connected with people who have helped me grow. The diversity of these people makes my life richer. I have always been open to others' thoughts and try not to judge them in any way.

The international movement for equality – across race, gender and beyond – has brought out the best, worst and, in some cases, continued silence of people. I liked and shared some content from one of my favourite cricket players and now commentator, Michael Holding. He was the voice of my decade of summers in England, commentating test matches. At the beginning of the 2020 test series with the West Indies, he shared his thoughts about the Black Lives Matter movement. They were raw and confronting. I found his viewpoint compelling and educational, so I shared it on social media.

Over a week or so, I was trolled by someone. The trolling began sarcastically and then slowly escalated to the point that I had to act. In the past, this person had been confronting, made me think, and provided a different perspective. But now, their approach was no longer respectful, and so I unfriended and blocked them.

In doing so, I recognise that I removed an opportunity to consider a different perspective. However, I could no longer tolerate such a divisive viewpoint. Divisions are destructive; they often entrench a group perspective that is potentially galvanising. This is not ideal, and, in some way, I added to the division by unfriending this person.

When did these recent divisions start?

Our interconnected, changing world has seen more humans severely impacted by specific events, such as the 2008 global financial crisis and, more recently, the COVID-19 pandemic. Many people feel increasingly uncertain and displaced. Research indicates that when people feel lost, they are likely to take a risk with their voting. In other words, many 'moderate' voters are turning to right-wing parties, particularly those at the extreme end of the scale.

Many of these parties are built on the concepts of nationalism and/or populism. In 2018, as many as twenty populist leaders held executive offices. This is the outcome of risk-loving voters. Some analysts have reported on how these right-wing parties will forge alliances with others around the world if re-elected. In a 2018 academic paper titled 'Is Nationalism on the Rise? Assessing Global Trends', author Florian Bieber (a Luxembourgian political scientist, historian and professor), states, 'Nationalism is based on distinguishing between members of the own nation, the in-group, and others, the out-group.'

According to Bieber, one way to measure the strength of this distinction is trust. Specifically, whether members of one nation trust members of other nations. He states, '*Data drawn from the World Value Survey between 2004 and 2014 suggest that the levels of citizens who do not (very much or at all) trust people from other nationalities vary greatly, from relatively low levels of distrust in multinational immigrant societies* [such] *as the United States, Australia and Argentina to high levels in Thailand or Morocco.'*

There is a difference between living in Australia and London, and I often remind my children of our community in London. This community was very diverse, with many people in our building from all corners of the globe. We lived in harmony and would celebrate the different cultural practices in gatherings during the year, with a keen interest in learning all about them. Although the UK voted to leave the EU, sixty per cent of Londoners wanted to stay. In 2020, one 'remain' voter from London referred to Brexit as *'the worst thing that will ever happen to this country.'* Speaking to CNBC, he went on to say, *'I think we'll live to regret it in a few years' time...My mum voted to exit* [the EU], *as did a lot of the older generation, and it's caused a massive rift for all of us.'*

Am I now writing this content based on a bias? Are you reading it with bias?

Many of the voting risk-takers are members of my peer group – white, middle-aged men. I speak with lots of these men regularly in my work. They are searching for something, and some of them are angry. They feel a little lost and maybe even a little scared. Since I founded my own advisory business in early 2019, I have been contacted by multiple middle-aged men. Often, they want to know how I went about launching my own business, as they are not confident about their tenure of employment.

Many middle-aged men feel the pressure to stay relevant – as they navigate an increasingly Gen Y-dominated workplace and an increased commitment to diversity. Often, these middle-aged men are not sharing what they are really thinking for fear of judgement or recrimination. I have sat in rooms where senior people have referred to this group as stale, frail and so on. The middle-aged men in the room tend to remain silent. But silence does not mean acceptance.

Men will talk privately among themselves, often seeking reassurance regarding their place in the world. Many have chosen not to share their experiences and thoughts more broadly because they are concerned about saying something 'wrong'. This suppression of opinion is one of the factors that may lead to 'risky' or 'shock' voting, as men become increasingly desperate to be heard and to feel validated – even if it means voting for a political party with extreme views.

Desperation or aggrieved entitlement?

'People who are given whatever they want soon develop a sense of entitlement and rapidly lose their sense of proportion.'

– Sarah Churchwell

Michelle: I absolutely agree that middle-aged men face increasing pressure to remain relevant in what is fast becoming a younger, more diverse and, in my opinion, more dynamic workplace. But isn't that just proof of another cycle in motion? You cannot be on top forever – whether that's at work, in politics or on the sporting field. Sooner or later, someone younger – who might not look the way you do – is going to oust you. It will not necessarily be hostile, but it is inevitable.

As for the argument that desperation can lead to risky voting, yes, absolutely. But I do not think desperation is the only driving force. In the case of Trump, for example, he was able to tap into an entire demographic of men who were not just feeling desperate but frustrated and pissed off.

Michael Kimmel sums it up perfectly in his book *Angry White Men*. (The book was first published in 2013 and republished in 2017, with a new preface devoted specifically to Trump.) According to Kimmel, '*white men's anger comes from the potent fusion of two sentiments – entitlement and a sense of victimisation.*' He states:

> '*The righteous indignation, the anti-Washington populism, is fuelled by what I came to call "aggrieved entitlement" – that sense that those benefits to which you believed yourself entitled have been snatched away from you...It might be hard for white men to realise that, irrespective of other factors, we have been running with the wind at our backs all these years and that what we think of as "fairness" to us has been built on the backs of others.*
>
> '*Ironically, that sense of being entitled is a marker not of depravation but of privilege. Those who have nothing don't feel they deserve anything; those who already have something believe they are entitled to it. When one feels that slipping, one may idealise...that earlier time when privilege was unexamined and assumed, and rage at those who seem to be taking what you thought was rightfully yours....Aggrieved entitlement can mobilise one politically, but it is often a mobilisation toward the past, not the future, to restore that which one feels has been lost.*'

This ties in with what David said earlier about the increasing number of voters longing for the past.

Kimmel goes on to argue that, despite claims to the contrary, gender and racial equality not only benefit racial minorities and women but also white people and men. The biggest benefactors, though, are children – *all* children. So, rather than 'speak out' by way of risky voting, men are encouraged to embrace the changes taking place around them:

'Make no mistake: the future...is more inclusive, more diverse, and more egalitarian. The choice for these men is not whether they can stem the tide; they cannot...The choice is whether they will be dragged kicking and screaming into that inevitable future or walk openly and honourably into it, far happier and healthier incidentally.'

Reflection

David: We began this chapter by discussing democracy, voting, men and the global shifts that are occurring in relation to these topics. These shifts have occurred over the past decade and will continue to influence our communities. My middle-aged male peer group appears to be contributing to the rise of populist leaders, for example. As technology continues to target communities with bias, will our governments act swiftly on this? Or will it be left to individuals? Awareness and education among us is likely to help avert undesirable situations.

When reflecting on this chapter, consider:

- Are you registered to vote? Why or why not?
- How deeply do you think about whom you vote for?
- What factors influence whom you vote for? Why are they important? How will they serve the future?
- Which online communities are you a member of? Do these communities expand or validate your thinking?
- What local community activities do you participate in? Do these expose you to different perspectives?
- With regard to social media, what are you sharing or commenting on? Why does this content appear in your news feed?
- Do you long for the past? Which aspects of the past do you believe will serve the future?

- What are you doing to contribute to a future that will be better than the past?
- What do you think we missed or skimmed over in this chapter? How could you step back further to consider other points that are interconnected or interdependent?

CHAPTER 2

Australia's Short-Termism

'I love Australia – I think.'

– Barry Humphries

Michelle: In this chapter, David and I turn our focus to our home country, Australia. Based on our research and experiences, we believe Australian governments and leaders have a tendency towards short-termism, often favouring what is popular or easy rather than what is best for the nation. This problem extends beyond the political sphere to the economy and the environment. David highlights the extent to which Australia's short-termism is hurting productivity, while I touch on another, perhaps more pressing area where Australia continues to lag: addressing climate change.

Australian prime ministership is a short-term gig

'Governments, especially democratic ones, are short-term and nationalistic.'

– Peter Senge

David: In August of 2018, Australia announced its fifth prime minister in as many years. As a result of this short-termism, I have lost some faith in Australian politics. We elect a party and, by extension, a leader – the Prime Minister of Australia. For me, that leader is intended to remain the same for the duration of the term.

However, popularity polls are taken regularly, and, in many instances, a leader who loses popularity is replaced rather than supported. This just does not feel right; it stinks of a quick fix, and I think sets a poor example for all Australians. The process to enable a leadership change is relatively simple. A leadership 'challenge' can be launched within the party on a Monday, a vote occurs on a Tuesday, and then suddenly on Wednesday there is a new prime minister.

The United Kingdom has also changed prime ministers at a similar rate in recent years, with David Cameron resigning in light of the Brexit vote, Theresa May resigning after failing to obtain the right terms to leave the EU, and Boris Johnson (the former London mayor and a schoolmate of David Cameron's) taking on the responsibility to leave the EU. These leadership changes have been more significant than those that have occurred in Australia, so I can accept them a little easier.

The Australian political landscape lost my attention after Kevin Rudd rolled Julia Gillard, who replaced Rudd initially. These replacements were based on polls and not policy execution. They lack the substance of the UK example, which at least is bound by a significant theme (whether Britain should leave or remain in the EU). When Kevin Rudd returned as prime minister, I felt sorry for my daughters, simply because it meant the end of a very short-lived term for Australia's first female prime minister.

In 2019, while appearing on the ABC's *Q&A* program, former Liberal Party leader John Hewson said:

> *'The system has become sort of inward looking and self-absorbed. The sort of people who get preselected these days*

are not necessarily those who will make good ministers. The skills you need to get through the factional process to be preselected in any of the major parties are not skills that will help you run a multibillion-dollar portfolio. We're getting the wrong people.'

I have met several federal ministers during my career. During each of these interactions, I was genuinely pleased and impressed by everyone's commitment to serving their country. However, you can't help but think that when a politician enters Canberra and gets swept up in party politics, a 'clean frog' jumps into the political pond and their priorities shift. It leaves you wondering whether the obsession with 'beating' the other side takes precedence over what is best for the nation.

It's about winning, not serving

'Success is always temporary. When all is said and done, the only thing you'll have left is your character.'

– Vince Gill

Michelle: As a child of the 90s, I grew up listening to the carefully considered musings of John Howard, who became almost like a grandfatherly figure – always there in the background, offering sage advice, whether you wanted it or not. It had never really occurred to me that his time in politics – or anyone else's time in politics, for that matter – was limited. But that is the nature of the game, isn't it? Sooner or later, the voting public outgrows you. Or it is simply ready for a change.

That was very much the case with Kevin 07, who seemed to glide in, seemingly out of nowhere (it always feels that way with opposition leaders, at least to me) and – with his sugary soundbites and carefully combed hair – swept into power.

John Howard was elected in 1996, when I was nine. People were still having 'election parties' back then – because to be voted in as prime minister actually meant something (like, not being ousted when the water looked a little choppy). When Rudd beat Howard ten years later, I was nineteen and studying journalism at university.

I distinctly remember crying into my glass of wine at my parents' place. Not so much because Howard had lost, but because it felt so *swift*. One minute, you are the leader of the country. The next minute, you are giving your concession speech in some half-full conference room, surrounded by a few forlorn-looking banners and balloons, and ashen faces. Of course, this is democracy in action. But that does not mean it isn't sad.

I could never have predicted what would come next: Rudd. Gillard. Rudd. Abbott. Turnbull. Morrison. Six prime ministers in fourteen years. What sort of message does this send to the younger generations of Australians – many of whom are already disenchanted with the political process, despite not even being allowed to vote yet?! Is this what we want Australian democracy to look like? A type of frantic merry-go-round, from which you can lose your spot at a moment's notice?

It goes back to the overarching theme of this book: our obsession to be 'better' than our peer. To 'beat' our competitor. To 'win' the game, at all costs (which, in the case of the Australian prime ministership, is the welfare of an entire country). At the ripe old age of thirty-three, I am tired of Australian politics. I still consider it a privilege to vote. I just hope the next prime minister I vote for sees out their term in full.

Australia's most trusted politician?
A New Zealander PM

'Public service is about serving all the people,
including the ones who are not like you.'

– Constance Wu

David: In 2019, Jacinda Ardern was declared the most trusted politician in Australia. The 2019 Believability Index asked participants to rate twelve politicians on six measures related to their 'believability':

- Relevance: Is in touch with the issues and things that matter to me.
- Integrity: Has strong principles and is driven by an ethical compass.
- Shared values: Reflects my beliefs and social/political priorities and values.
- Commitment: Has my community's best interests at heart.
- Affinity: A person I can relate to and like.
- Follow through: Delivers on their promises, does what they say they will.

Jacinda Ardern scored seventy-seven out of 100. The next politician, Penny Wong, scored fifty-three, followed by Julie Bishop at fifty-two and then Tanya Plibersek at fifty. The first male politician was Anthony Albanese at number five, with a score of forty-six.

Ardern was re-elected in a landslide win in 2020, with a policy agenda referred to as not being left or right but in the middle. This was the first parliamentary majority since New Zealand's Mixed Member Proportional (MMP) voting system was introduced in 1996. It was adopted from West Germany, and is deliberately designed to avoid majorities and encourage coalitions. On the evening of the election, Ardern was explicit about her plan to govern for unity. It was not for her Labour Party's traditional believers, but for middle New Zealand. For many years, Labour's vote came from urban centres, and it still does, but the swing in provincial seats and rural seats was huge.

Beyond her party's policies, Ardern has managed some challenging situations and has endeared herself to the public. In 2020, Ardern eradicated community transmission of COVID-19 in New Zealand. Before that, she led a compassionate response to the Christchurch mosque shootings, gaining global admiration, was the second PM to have a baby while in office (the late Pakistani prime minister Benazir Bhutto was the first), and took her infant into the chamber of the United Nations General Assembly.

Watching Jacinda Ardern communicate reminds me of a course on leadership storytelling that I attended in Surrey in the United Kingdom. My colleagues and I were required to deliver messages to one another, practising our delivery to our peer group and external facilitator. We learned of a storytelling formula designed to 'take people with you'. Great leaders throughout history, when addressing their people, begin with the past, explain the 'today', and share an aspirational vision of the future. These three simple phases offer opportunities to pause and deliver the key points with the appropriate level of intensity. I have observed Jacinda Ardern applying the formula multiple times while remaining genuine.

An article by NBC News suggests Ardern's down-to-earth style is made possible in New Zealand because of the country's 'intimate democracy' – a term coined by Harshan Kumarasingham, a New Zealander who teaches politics at the University of Edinburgh in Scotland. He states, 'It's normal here to have "normal people" as prime ministers.'

Is Australia over-governed?

*'Simplicity does not precede
complexity, but follows it.'*

– Alan Perlis

David: In 2011, at a fancy Melbourne restaurant on Collins Street, I attended a company dinner, which was also attended by a very well-known, long-serving, successful politician. My British colleague asked him about the challenges of being an Australian politician. It became apparent that there are several differences to the UK political system, like the streaming of individuals into state or federal politics, and the influence the states have on federal policy. The state border closures due to COVID-19 are a prime example of the latter. The federal government sought a national, coordinated approach, yet the states took matters into their own hands, resulting in inconsistencies and public confusion.

The complexity of the Australian government – including the infighting within parties and the fact that the federal government is, in some respects, pitted against the states (which are also pitted against each other) – creates an imbalance. In 2017, former Australian prime minister the late Bob Hawke called for state governments to be abolished. Speaking at Queensland's Woodford Festival, he said:

> *'What we have today – as I have said before – basically represents the meanderings of British explorers across the Australian continent more than 200 years ago. They wandered around and lines were drawn on a map and jurisdiction and governance followed.*

> *'So you have 13 parliaments* [including senates] *dealing with much the same issues and I believe that the simple fact*

is the states should be abolished. I raised that with my own colleagues and...they are not overly keen on it. So many comfortable seats to put bums on in parliaments all over this country, but it seems to be that that is what ought to happen.'

I am not the only one who thinks this idea has some merit. According to a 2017 article in *The Conversation,* the reason Australia has a federal constitution is due to fear. The colonies were fearful of domination by each other or by the new national government. But the Australian government – in its current form – is complex and expensive. The same article states that in 2002, the annual cost of federalism to the economy was an estimated $40 billion.

A federal budget paper, titled 'Australian Government funding to the states', reveals that, in aggregate, the states were estimated to receive Australian government payments of $127.4 billion in 2019–20. Total payments to the states in 2019–20 were estimated to be 25.4 per cent of total Australian government expenditure and account for about 44.6 per cent of total state revenue. Australian government payments effectively support about forty-six per cent of state expenditure, as shown in the following table. (Note that this table refers to data from 2017–18.) The federal and state governments have departments that replicate one another and set different policies, and I suspect governments do business with themselves.

Australian government's contribution to state expenditure

2017-18	Australian Government tied payments $million	State spending supported by general revenue assistance(b) $million	Total state spending $million	State spending supported by Australian Government revenue per cent
Education	20,607	12,658	61,298	54.3
Health	20,437	17,439	76,498	49.5
Housing and community amenities	2,128	1,889	8,199	49.0
Transport	6,974	6,261	27,100	48.8
Social protection	2,555	6,328	22,898	38.8
Other functions(a)	3,408	19,622	66,487	34.6
Payments for specific purpose	56,107			
General revenue assistance		64,197		
Total			262,480	45.8

Source: Australian Government and state government Final Budget Outcomes for 2017-18.

Note that 2017-18 data on an ABS Classification of the Functions of Government (COFOG-A) basis is unavailable for the Australian Government and Victoria. Australian Government and Victorian expense by purpose date has been adjusted to align with COFOG-A

(a) 'Other functions' includes additional functions not elsewhere itemised but does not include general revenue assistance

(b) General revenue assistance (GRA) is provided to the States without conditions, to spend according to their own budget priorities. For illustrative purposes GRA is allocated to expense functions based on the ratio of discretionary spending in each function as a share of states' total discretionery spending.

There is potentially an indirect cost, too, as many people, including Michelle and myself, have checked out of Australian politics due to the infighting. Australia has nine governments and fifteen legislative chambers for a population of 25.5 million. Is this what we now require?

Interestingly, the late Bob Hawke and I are not alone in this view. According to a 2014 survey commissioned by Beyond Federation, thirty-nine per cent of the Australian population think the state governments should be abolished. This was higher than the number of people who were opposed (thirty-one per cent) and those who were undecided (thirty per cent). The survey states, *'Although those in favour of abolishing State governments outnumber those opposed, the large number of those undecided and the tendency for voters to prefer to maintain the status quo means that a referendum on the issue would be unlikely to be carried at the present point in time.'*

If Australia were to have a single set of laws governing the entire country – like New Zealand and the United Kingdom, both of which have a single national parliament – it would mean one department of education, agriculture, environment and so on. The disputes over shares of Commonwealth revenue allocated to the states would be no more, and expenditure would be based on the needs of the people.

In an opinion piece for *The Age* titled 'Enough of the short-term politics – we need a government that leads', John Hewson highlights a range of issues within the current Australian government. According to Hewson, there is a lot of talk but not enough action, citing failed promises regarding drought and bushfire assistance, plus a series of scandals on both sides of politics over several decades, and the efforts to downplay them and cover them up.

After committing to establish a National Integrity Commission, it took two years for a bill to be produced to that effect, only for its proposal to lack integrity. The article states, '*Careful legal assessment suggests the proposed commission would operate as a protection racket for politicians and their staff.*' The culminative effect is the erosion of voter trust. Hewson concludes, '*Voters want good government. They have had enough of short-term politics.*'

According to Ralph Ashton, who, in 2012, co-founded the Australian Futures Project in a bid to understand and address Australia's short-termism, it is high time we rewrote the rulebook. In a 2018 article for *The Sydney Morning Herald*, Ashton said:

> '*It's almost 120 years since the ground rules for Australia were set at Federation. The world has changed dramatically and Australia's system for making important decisions hasn't kept up. It's like there's a bunch of new hardware and software but Australia hasn't updated its operating system.*'

The technology analogy resonates with someone like me, as my work with organisations often means identifying and reviewing different options. Some of these options are uncomfortable for the recipients, especially when they are impacted directly, but not owning or benefiting from the change. There are difficult conversations to be had before exploring these options, and this is even before any possible shortlist for selection. The conversation often begins with the education of those who are not familiar with alternatives.

Similarly, if there is any possibility of a change to how Australia is governed, we need to consider the public's exposure to, and understanding of, alternative models working in other areas of the world.

Australian short-termism is hurting productivity

'Productivity is being able to do things that you were never able to do before.'

– Franz Kafka

David: The leadership of a country has an influence on the culture of businesses that operate within that country. Within the Asia-Pacific region, Australia is a large country with a small population, which is focused on doing business within itself. Unfortunately, the parochial nature of many Australian businesses – combined with the country's tendency for short-termism – has ultimately led to a decline in productivity, which, if left unaddressed, could have devastating consequences.

Change in productivity per hour worked, 1970 to 2017

Labour productivity per hour is measured as gross domestic product (GDP) per hour of work.
GDP is adjusted for price differences between countries (PPP adjustment) and for price changes over time (inflation).

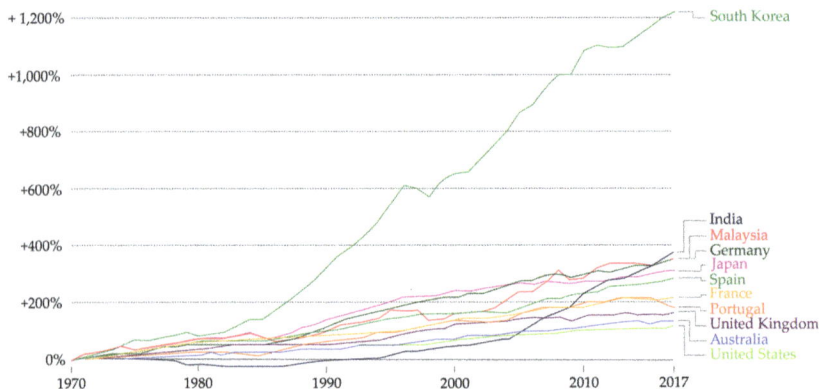

Source: Our World in Data

Economically speaking, many people think Australia is, by and large, doing well. However, productivity data shows this may not be the case. According to an article by my favourite Australian newspaper, *The Age*, we are stuck in a state of akrasia. When I first read that word, I thought it was another slang word created by an Australian with some reference to our role in Asia. Well, it is not. Per the Oxford Lexico, Akrasia is *'the state of mind in which someone acts against their better judgement through weakness of will'*.

When done in the right way, taking a longer-term perspective can lead to huge benefits. A former employer of mine was an exceptionally well-regarded organisation with a long history. This history also carried some legacy practices, some of which are no longer applicable in this century. The organisation's CEO was charismatic and exceptionally clever; he knew that any change to be expected within the organisation had to be understood and carried forward by the people.

He mandated simple presentations, two-page papers and everything written in a clear, straightforward way. The understanding of complex topics, and the level of quality dialogue and sound decision making, improved across the entire organisation in the following months. He also helped change our mindset, taking a longer-term perspective with a strapline for the change programs of '1,000 days for 100 years'. Powerful stuff. I have been involved in many change efforts within many organisations, and this statement remains the strongest for me.

Australia is a wealthy country with a world-class healthcare system, yet, according to the article, more than a third of the combined federal and state health budgets are spent on treating preventable illnesses like obesity and diabetes. Did you know that? This is another example of a cycle we are stuck in, only addressing symptoms and not the root cause.

In a bid to change this, Ralph Ashton has met with more than 1,000 leaders across Australian society *'to work out ways to end this logjam while ensuring Australia's continued prosperity.'* This includes politicians, public servants, community leaders, chief executives, heads of think tanks and charities, vice-chancellors and academics, and senior editors, journalists and opinion-makers.

As Mr Ashton explained in the article:

> *'I asked four questions. Is there really a problem with short-termism in Australia? The response was a unanimous yes. Is this problem any different from other times in Australia's 230-year history? Yes, again. It's the worst in living memory. What can be done about it? Only 2 per cent of the leaders I spoke to had concrete suggestions. You read that right: only about 20 of the 1000 leaders had tangible ideas.*

'There's no one simple fix. Improvement will come from a messy mix of immediate gains in specific parts of the system, slow system-wide changes, and some failure along the way. It will involve work from the top-down (government, big business, established civil society organisations) as well as the bottom-up (grassroots action and engaging the public at large). Patience and tenacity are required.'

Mr Ashton has lived and worked in dozens of countries around the world. Like me, he believes Australia could benefit from trialling solutions without an expectation of success. This will require curiosity and humility to understand and consider how the country could break out of this cycle. This will challenge the bravado, 'she'll be right' attitude that so many Australians have towards life. After all, Australia is known as the 'Lucky Country', enjoying a twenty-eight-year recession-free run until the outbreak of COVID-19. Now more than ever, Australia needs to shake off its short-termism tendencies and overhaul its piecemeal approach to progress.

Other reasons why Australian productivity is lagging

'Human decision-making is complex. On our own, our tendency to yield to short-term temptations, and even to addictions, may be too strong for our rational, long-term planning.'

– Peter Singer

David: There are other contributing factors that help to explain why Australia is falling behind other countries, in an economic sense. According to research conducted by the MIT Center for Information Systems Research (at the MIT Sloan School of Management), only three per cent of Australian businesses are future-ready, compared to twenty-two per cent globally. Future-ready firms reported 19.3 per cent higher margins and 26.6 per cent higher growth than their industry averages.

The research also reveals that seventy-nine per cent of Australian businesses (compared to fifty-one per cent globally) remain in the pre-transformed state of 'silos and spaghetti', in the sense that they still have a traditional structure with regard to their customer experience and operational efficiency.

The research is consistent with the views of Australian Treasury Deputy Secretary Meghan Quinn, who, in a speech given at the OECD Global Forum on Productivity in June 2019, said sluggish wage and productivity growth is being exacerbated by the failure of Australian businesses to embrace disruptive technologies at the same rate as many of their global peers.

Interestingly, Ms Quinn said mining and energy firms have been better than companies in other sectors at infusing new technologies into their workplaces, benefiting productivity. However, other industries are slipping behind. '*Treasury analysis suggests that labour productivity in the non-mining sector could increase by 6 per cent if managerial practices rose to those in the mining sector,*' Ms Quinn said.

In an interview with *The Australian Financial Review*, Ms Quinn said while many firms may be investing in emerging technologies, such as artificial intelligence, cloud computing and blockchain, they could be using new technologies more effectively.

When I was living in London in 2008, and the global financial crisis began to bite, it was evident that something had changed. During the week, there were more fathers in parks, spending time with their young children. Meanwhile, apartment rents and values had fallen quickly in central London. The system was effectively being cleansed, and people were forced to change jobs – sometimes entering an entirely new sector.

Compare this to Australia's twenty-eight-year recession-free run, which meant far less job movement or the need for companies to reinvent themselves. The Australian Treasury estimates that a one per cent decrease in the job switching rate is roughly associated with a 0.5 per cent decline in wages growth. The rate of job switching by workers has fallen to eight per cent, from eleven per cent in the early 2000s. '*Much of this decline appears to reflect a reduction in worker transitions from mature to young firms,*' Ms Quinn said.

The rate of entry for employing firms has also declined in recent years, falling from fourteen per cent in the early 2000s to eleven per cent in recent years. Said Ms Quinn, '*We know that a fall in firm entry is generally bad news for job creation and technology adoption. Low-productivity firms are also increasingly surviving, further impeding resource reallocation to more productive firms.*'

Overall, labour productivity growth has averaged 1.1 per cent per year over the past five years – which is better than the OECD average of 0.9 per cent. However, this is well below Australia's productivity growth rate of 1.7 per cent in the mid-1970s.

What could be contributing to this?

According to Ms Quinn, a slowdown in capital investment by business, known as 'capital shallowing'. While the mining industry has the capital to invest, other industries are potentially swept up in Australia's short-termism, manifesting in capital shallowing. RBA governor Philip Lowe has appealed to government and business to focus on reforms that lift productivity to improve the economy's growth potential.

Quinn believes the community also has a role to play, stating, '*The steps for government, business and the community more broadly to impact productivity include building the evidence base for reform; agreeing on priorities for policy; strengthening reform partnerships at different levels of government and among the community; and effectively managing any transitional costs that may arise.*'

Australia's climate change shame

*'For Australians, climate change
is no longer a distant threat.'*

– Kevin Rudd

Michelle: Australian short-termism extends beyond the economy, of course. It can also be seen across social and cultural parameters, as well as Australia's wishy-washy approach to addressing climate change. According to the 2020 Climate Change Performance Index, Australia is the sixth worst performing country of the fifty-seven countries assessed (across four key categories of emissions, renewable energy, energy use and climate policy), trailing behind a long list of less developed nations including Thailand, Indonesia, Algeria and Kazakhstan.

Overall results of the 2020 Climate Change Performance Index

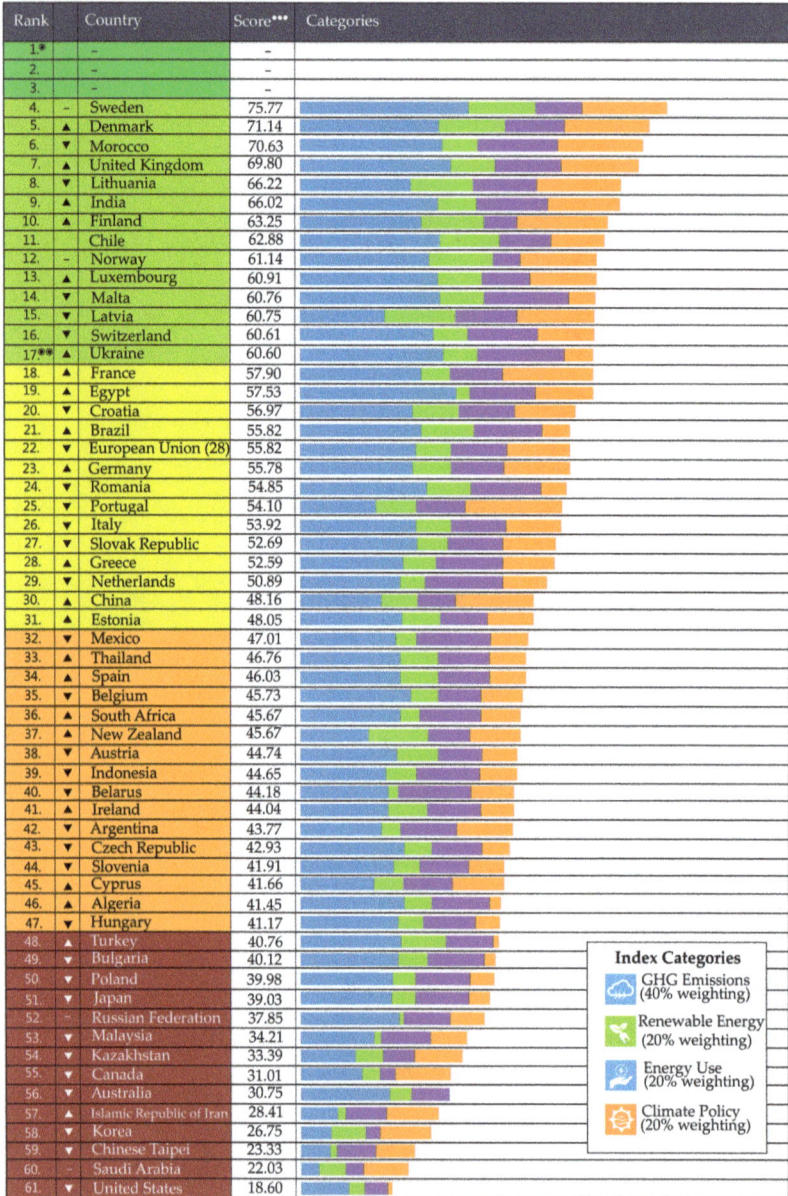

Rank		Country	Score***	Categories
1.*	–	–	–	
2.		–	–	
3.		–	–	
4.	–	Sweden	75.77	
5.	▲	Denmark	71.14	
6.	▼	Morocco	70.63	
7.	▲	United Kingdom	69.80	
8.	▼	Lithuania	66.22	
9.	▲	India	66.02	
10.	▲	Finland	63.25	
11.		Chile	62.88	
12.	–	Norway	61.14	
13.	▲	Luxembourg	60.91	
14.	▼	Malta	60.76	
15.	▼	Latvia	60.75	
16.	▼	Switzerland	60.61	
17**	▲	Ukraine	60.60	
18.	▲	France	57.90	
19.	▲	Egypt	57.53	
20.	▼	Croatia	56.97	
21.	▲	Brazil	55.82	
22.	▼	European Union (28)	55.82	
23.	▲	Germany	55.78	
24.	▼	Romania	54.85	
25.	▼	Portugal	54.10	
26.	▼	Italy	53.92	
27.	▼	Slovak Republic	52.69	
28.	▲	Greece	52.59	
29.	▼	Netherlands	50.89	
30.	▲	China	48.16	
31.	▲	Estonia	48.05	
32.	▼	Mexico	47.01	
33.	▲	Thailand	46.76	
34.	▲	Spain	46.03	
35.	▼	Belgium	45.73	
36.	▲	South Africa	45.67	
37.	▲	New Zealand	45.67	
38.	▼	Austria	44.74	
39.	▼	Indonesia	44.65	
40.	▼	Belarus	44.18	
41.	▲	Ireland	44.04	
42.	▼	Argentina	43.77	
43.	▼	Czech Republic	42.93	
44.	▼	Slovenia	41.91	
45.	▲	Cyprus	41.66	
46.	▲	Algeria	41.45	
47.	▼	Hungary	41.17	
48.	▲	Turkey	40.76	
49.	▼	Bulgaria	40.12	
50.	▼	Poland	39.98	
51.	▼	Japan	39.03	
52.	–	Russian Federation	37.85	
53.	▼	Malaysia	34.21	
54.	▼	Kazakhstan	33.39	
55.	▼	Canada	31.01	
56.	▼	Australia	30.75	
57.	▲	Islamic Republic of Iran	28.41	
58.	▼	Korea	26.75	
59.	▼	Chinese Taipei	23.33	
60.	–	Saudi Arabia	22.03	
61.	▼	United States	18.60	

Index Categories
- GHG Emissions (40% weighting)
- Renewable Energy (20% weighting)
- Energy Use (20% weighting)
- Climate Policy (20% weighting)

Source: 2020 Climate Change Performance Index

(According to the report, no countries achieved positions 1-3, as no country is doing enough to prevent dangerous climate change.)

Alarmingly, the report states, '*Australia receives the lowest rating in this year's Climate Policy rating as experts observe that the newly elected government has continued to worsen performance at both national and international levels.*' Describing the Australian government as '*an increasingly regressive force*', the report criticised its failure to '*clarify how it will meet the country's insufficient 2030 emission reduction target and inaction in developing a long-term mitigation strategy.*'

In a 2019 interview with *Guardian Australia*, former prime minister Malcolm Turnbull said the Liberal Party had struggled with climate change denialism since 2007. He has reportedly been told that companies were avoiding Australia because of the lack of policy and because of political risk.

Foreign companies are not the only ones giving Australia a wider berth, it seems. In 2019, Sweden's central bank said it had sold off bonds from Australia and Queensland because it felt that Australia's greenhouse gas emissions were too high. It is worth noting that Sweden topped the charts in the 2020 Climate Change Performance Index. In the report, Sweden was commended for its strong climate policy framework, including its 2045 net-zero emission target (previously set for 2050), the world's highest carbon tax and a 100 per cent renewable energy target by 2040.

Australia's poor performance in relation to climate change should not come as a surprise. What may surprise you, however, is the impact this is having on Australians. According to a 2018 report published by the University of Melbourne, climate change is the number one concern among members of Generation X (David's generation) and Generation Y (my generation). The report is part of the Life Patterns research program, which is '*designed to follow patterns in people's lives over time in order to gain a longitudinal and holistic understanding of the ways in which two generations of Australians are responding to our rapidly changing world*'.

When asked to nominate the most important issues facing Australia, the participants' responses tended to reflect their life stage. For example, among members of Gen X, some of the most important issues were the cost of living, security and terrorism, education and the economy. Among members of Gen Y, some of the most important issues were the lack of jobs/job security, drug abuse, housing affordability and health.

But there was one area that *both* groups identified as their *main* concern: the environment.

What issues do Gen X and Gen Y care about most?

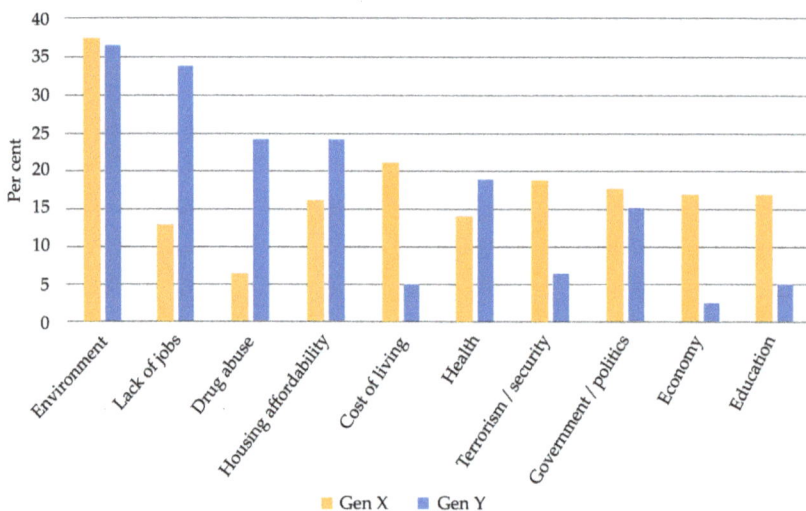

Source: 'Examining the most important issues in Australia: similarities and differences across two generations' (The University of Melbourne)

The report states, '*Participants from both cohorts used a range of terms to talk about the environment. The terms "environment" and "environmental concerns" were used interchangeably with "climate change", often by the same participant, suggesting that they viewed these issues as equivalent.*' Several participants in each group identified the lack of action or leadership on environment issues or climate change as the root of their concern, with one participant describing it as '*a crying shame*'.

By failing to address climate change in a real and dedicated fashion, the Australian government is not only alienating foreign entities but alienating its own people too. This comes back to Australia's overreliance on short-termism. At this point, we need much, much more than a quick fix. This is highlighted further in the next section.

Slow Decline versus Outlook Vision

*'I respectfully decline the invitation
to join your hallucination.'*

– Scott Adams

Michelle: The Australian National Outlook 2019, produced by the Commonwealth Scientific and Industrial Research Organisation (CSIRO) in conjunction with National Australia Bank, paints a sobering yet optimistic picture of Australia's future. The report combines CSIRO modelling and research with insights from more than fifty leaders across twenty-two leading Australian organisations. Over a two-year period, participants explored several possible outcomes for Australia.

In essence, Australia is at a crossroads. It can stride towards a more positive future outlook filled with growth or face a slow decline. The report states (my emphasis added):

> *'The research argues that it is possible to achieve higher GDP per capita (as much as 36%), while ensuring growth is inclusive and environmentally sustainable. In a global context, **strong co-operation on climate change and trade can deliver a better outcome for Australia without***

significantly impacting our economic growth, where before it may have been thought impossible.'

For this to happen, five core shifts are required in the following areas:

- **Industry** (to enable a productive, inclusive and resilient economy, with new strengths in both the domestic and export sectors).
- **Urban** (to enable well-connected, affordable cities that offer more equal access to quality jobs, lifestyle amenities, education and other services).
- **Energy** (to manage Australia's transition to a reliable, affordable, low-emissions energy economy that builds on Australia's existing sources of comparative advantage).
- **Land** (to create a profitable and sustainable mosaic of food, fibre and fuel production, carbon sequestration and biodiversity).
- **Culture** (to encourage more engagement, curiosity, collaboration and solutions, and which should be supported by inclusive civic and political institutions).

If these shifts do not occur, Australia is at risk of entering a 'Slow Decline' scenario, whereby economic growth, investment and education outcomes are all relatively weak, and the economy is increasingly vulnerable to external shocks. The report states, *'Although energy policy issues are resolved domestically, the low-emissions energy transmission is stymied by a lack of global cooperation on climate change. Both energy and agricultural productivity remain relatively low.'*

There are other problems in the Slow Decline scenario too:

In 'Slow Decline', Australia drifts into the future

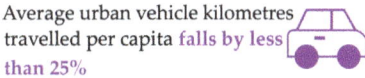

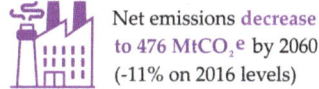

GDP grows at **2.1%** annually

Real wages are **40% higher** in 2060 than today

Cities sprawl with little change in density

Average urban vehicle kilometres travelled per capita falls by less than 25%

Net emissions decrease to 476 MtCO$_2$e by 2060 (-11% on 2016 levels)

61% increase in total energy use by 2060 (on 2016 levels), with only a modest improvement in energy productivity

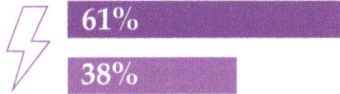

61%

38%

Households spend 38% less on electricity as a percentage of income

Returns to landholders increase by around **$18 billion** between 2016 and 2060

Minimal environmental plantings in 2060

Source: Australian National Outlook 2019

In the second scenario, titled Outlook Vision, Australia reaches its full potential. Economic growth remains strong and inclusive, as Australian companies use technology to move productivity '*towards the global frontier*' and create new globally competitive, export-facing industries. Importantly, Australia successfully transitions its energy system, delivering high reliability and affordability, and lower emissions. '*If the world cooperates to limit climate change to 2°C, Australia can go even further and reach "net zero" emissions by 2050, driven by significant shifts in land use to carbon plantings,*' the report states.

Here are some of the other benefits of the Outlook Vision scenario:

In the 'Outlook Vision', Australia reaches its full potential

GDP grows at **2.75-2.8%** annually

Real wages are **90% higher** in 2060 than today

Average density of major cities increases 60-88%

Average urban vehicle kilometres travelled per capita reduced by 33-45% with greater uptake of mass transit

Australia reaches net-zero emissions by 2050 under a cooperative global context, with the potential for net-negative emissions by 2060

6-28% increase in total energy use by 2060 (on 2016 levels) with more than a doubling of energy productivity per unit of GDP

6-28%

64%

Households spend up to 64% less on electricity as a percentage of income

Returns to landholders increase by **$42-84 billion** between 2016 and 2060

11-20 Mha of environmental plantings in 2060 under a cooperative global context (12-24% of intensive agricultural land)

Source: Australian National Outlook 2019

According to the report, there are three main points to consider in striving for the Outlook Vision scenario:

The upside is significant

In the Outlook Vision scenario, Australians benefit from significantly higher GDP, environmentally sustainable growth, energy affordability, high liveability and readily available access to services.

It's achievable across a range of global contexts

A key feature of the Outlook Vision scenario is strong global cooperation on trade and climate change. This will result in the best environmental outcomes without significantly affecting economic growth. But Australia must be willing to deal with the full range of possible global contexts.

It's within our grasp, but requires action and long-term thinking

While the Outlook Vision is possible, it will require action. As stated before, Australia will need to undergo five major shifts (across industry, urban, energy, land and culture). However, it is worth noting that one shift will positively impact others. And I believe that every Australian has an opportunity to influence at least one of these shifts – either professionally, within their community or even on an individual level.

Reflection

David: We opened the chapter by highlighting Australia's short-termism and the number of recent prime ministers. But it extends far beyond politics. Short-termism is hindering Australian productivity and the business sector, and our ability as a country to address climate change. This information is sobering, but not overly surprising. If Australia fails to act, the country risks entering a 'Slow Decline' scenario and will become more vulnerable to external shocks. The alternative is to act – with the appropriate use of technology to improve productivity, the transition of energy systems and the creation of a globally competitive, export-facing industry.

When reflecting on this chapter, consider:

- Do you agree that Australia suffers from a tendency towards short-termism? Why or why not?
- If you are an Australian, would you support a referendum on changing how we are governed? Why or why not?
- Do you think Australia is over-governed? Why or why not?
- Do you have an opinion on the decline in productivity in Australia?
- Have you ever experienced akrasia? What drove this?

- Do you have, or have you observed, the Australian attitude of 'she'll be right'? What could be the consequences of this?
- If you run a business, how does it compare to its global peers?
- What are the areas of technology vulnerability within your business or the organisation you work for? What are the consequences?
- What do you think of Australia's efforts to date to address climate change? What might we do differently?

PART 2

WORKPLACE

CHAPTER 3

The Global Village

'The global village is a place of very arduous interfaces and very abrasive situations.'

– Marshall McLuhan

Michelle: In this chapter, David and I touch on a range of challenges facing modern workplaces worldwide, including globalisation, digital burnout and death by overwork (yes, you read that right). We also highlight the allure of start-ups and entrepreneurship, particularly among young people, before offering some broader ideas about hierarchies within working environments.

The challenges of globalisation

'Globalisation will make our societies more creative and prosperous, but also more vulnerable.'

– Lord Robertson

David: The world continues to change. My business is all about change; the word 'change' is even in the name – CHANGE lead®. What I have found is that change is welcomed by those who initiate, manage or, dare I say, control it. If you ask people about change, they generally say that they are up for it. However, in most situations, they are only up for it if they can somehow control it.

In the workplace, one of the most significant changes we have seen is globalisation. This is the process by which businesses and other organisations develop international influence and/or start operating on an international scale.

Globalisation will continue to impact everyone around the world, in a variety of ways. These include changes in technology, the ability to access services across the world from the comfort of your home, and the ability to have goods delivered from anywhere around the globe. These changes have greatly impacted economies, communities and the environment. There are benefits, of course. For example, economies have become increasingly interdependent, helping global GDP grow from US$50 trillion in 2000 to US$75 trillion in 2016.

However, one of the challenges of globalisation is the uneven distribution of its benefits and costs. In 2017, Liu Zhenmin, Under-Secretary-General for the United Nations Department of Economic and Social Affairs (DESA), stated, *'To ensure that globalisation can be leveraged to support inclusive economic growth and sustainable development, it is essential to analyse the current system as well as emerging trends to devise policy solutions addressing them.'*

DESA has identified three mega-trends, or challenges, related to globalisation:

- Shifts in production and labour markets
- Rapid advances in technology
- Climate change

Shifts in production and labour markets

Production changes, including through outsourcing and mechanisation, have had a huge impact on labour markets, namely in the form of job losses, particularly in manufacturing. According to DESA, '*These trends in labour markets are associated with higher rates of income inequality, which has increased in a majority of countries across the globe.*'

Rapid advances in technology

The fast-moving development and advancement of new technologies – including in information and communications, and artificial intelligence – has significantly affected the world of work. DESA warns, '*While these innovations can act as catalysts for sustainable development, countries that do not have access to them are at risk of being left behind.*'

Climate change

The third emerging mega-trend is the effect of globalisation on climate change. As DESA states, '*many trends closely linked to globalisation, including economic activity, lifestyle changes and urbanisation, all have an impact on our environment and may contribute to climate change.*'

For globalisation to achieve sustainable development, it must work for all, said Mr Liu, stressing that global agreements can play a key role in strengthening the benefits of globalisation. Such agreements already include the 2030 Agenda for Sustainable Development, the Addis Ababa Action Agenda on Financing for Development, and the Paris Agreement on climate change. According to Mr Liu, the UN should continue to help member states devise country-specific policy approaches as well.

Death by overwork

'It can kind of screw up things if you're trying to overwork something.'

– Jeff Bridges

David: I have worked in international teams, with globalisation being an everyday business, and I really enjoyed it. Teams were aligned to geographies; other groups supported the data for these geographies. There were different demands within each of these businesses, including some culture practices that were not always practical. However, there were businesses always interested in understanding the activities of others, especially those businesses of a similar size. Country culture influenced how business was done, but it was the size of other similar types of businesses that offered opportunities to optimise how. It provided opportunities to optimise the local effort. However, it is unlikely that all companies are able or willing to operate like this.

Globalisation allows access to labour markets that may not be as regulated as the country where an organisation is headquartered. For example, Chinese manufacturing employees are known for working long hours, often in risky environments. But now it seems the long-hours culture has spread to China's office workers. This is partly due to the country's burgeoning tech sector.

According to a 2019 article in the *Financial Times*, staff at tech companies often use the phrase '996' to describe their working hours. That is, starting work at 9am, leaving at 9pm and working six days a week. The article, which cites statistics from the 2017 China Labour Dynamics Survey, states that the average Chinese employee spends 44.7 hours a week at work. More than forty per cent of survey respondents reported working longer than fifty hours per week.

The article states, '*The question of overwork among Chinese white-collar workers, in the tech industry in particular, became a talking point in 2016 when Zhang Rui, the 44-year-old founder of a mobile health app start-up, died suddenly of a heart attack. Chinese media reports linked his death to his punishing routine of working late into the night – often still sending emails at 3am.*'

In China, death by overwork is a recognised concept. It even has a name – 'guolaosi'. In many eastern Asian countries, such as China, it is common for businessmen in particular to work long hours – and then feel the pressure of expanding and pleasing their networks. Making these connections is called building 'guanxi'. It is important for businessmen to broaden their guanxi relationships, especially with powerful officials or bosses. But at what cost? The *Financial Times* article states:

'*People who work for more than 55 hours a week face an increased risk of stroke and coronary heart disease compared with those who work between 35 and 40 hours a week, according to a study based on data from more than 600,000 individuals...A survey in Shanghai [in 2018] of patients with cardiovascular disease found a significant incidence of arrhythmia – an irregular heartbeat that can be a prelude to more serious disease – in patients aged 21 to 30. Sun Baogui, executive vice-chairman of the Chinese Heart Failure Society, says this finding was consistent with their reported lifestyle of long working hours and getting little sleep.*'

Mental health is another risk. The same article cites a 2017 Kantar Health survey, which found nearly twenty per cent of adults in China who worked more than fifty-one hours a week reported feelings of anxiety. As China continues to expand its reach internationally, and grow its commercial influence, we can expect a larger portion of its professional workforce to spend more hours working. While some Chinese companies – like Nocode Technology, a medical research engine start-up – recognise that overworked employees do not achieve better results, more needs to be done to protect others from extreme overwork.

For example, the European Union has a directive that employees should work no more than 48 hours per week. On average, a full-time employee in the European Union works 40.3 hours per week in a usual working week. Denmark – with a working week of 37.8 hours – is the only country in the EU in which the normal number of working hours is less than 38. The next shortest week is in Italy (38.8), followed by the Netherlands and France (both 39), and Finland and Ireland (39.1). Meanwhile, full-time employees in the UK spend an average of 42.3 hours at their main job every week.

Many workers are also loath to take their annual leave. According to a 2017 Glassdoor survey, the average US employee had only taken about half of their paid time off in the past twelve months. However, researchers at University of California, Los Angeles (UCLA) have come up with a simple way to help address the problem of overwork and burnout: Treat your weekend as a holiday.

The researchers came to the unsurprising conclusion that holidays improve health, job performance and creativity. Their study involved two control groups over a particular weekend. The first group was told to treat the weekend as a regular one, while the second was told to think and behave as if they were on holiday.

The second group spent less time on housework, and more time eating and being with loved ones. As a result, they reported back to work on Monday happier than the first group. The researchers said it was the holiday *mindset* – rather than specific activities – that made all the difference:

> *'The benefits do not require taking additional time off from work, excessive spending for extravagant travel or the inclusion of particular activities. Fully attainable to anyone,*

vacations involve a mental break that allows people to become more fully engaged in and absorbed by their time off, making that time more enjoyable.'

Working smarter, not longer

'I feel many times we do all the hard work, but in the absence of smart work, we do not get the desired results.'

– Sandeep Singh

David: *'Work expands so as to fill the time available for its completion.'* This is the adage of Parkinson's Law, articulated by British naval historian and author Cyril Northcote Parkinson as part of an essay published in *The Economist* in 1955. It means that, if you give yourself a day to complete a one-hour task, then, psychologically speaking, the task will become more complex so as to fill the entire day. It goes without saying that this can be a major hindrance to productivity.

In the previous section, I spoke about China and the concerning trend of death by overwork. Japan faces the same problem. Japan has some of the longest working hours in the world. 'Karoshi' is a Japanese term to describe death by overwork.

According to a 2017 BBC article, nearly a quarter of Japanese companies have employees working more than eighty hours of overtime a month, while twelve per cent are working more than 100 hours of overtime a month. The article states, *'Those numbers are important; 80 hours overtime a month is regarded as the threshold above which you have an increased chance of dying.'* The article also states that while Japanese workers are entitled to twenty days of leave a year, about thirty-five per cent do not take any leave at all.

In 2019, Microsoft's Japanese subsidiary implemented a four-day workweek as part of an initiative known as the 'Work-Life Choice Challenge'. This initiative examined work-life balance and its effect on productivity and creativity. During the month of August, Microsoft Japan closed its offices every Friday, giving full-time employees paid leave during the closures. Beyond the office closure, the company also reduced meeting times by encouraging a thirty-minute time limit and encouraging more remote communication. The outcome was a forty per cent productivity increase when compared to August 2018.

Presumably, the Work-Life Choice Challenge was designed to challenge some of the cultural norms around overwork in Japan. But Microsoft Japan is not the only one to consider a shorter workweek – and see the upside. In 2019, New Zealand company Perpetual Guardian moved permanently to a four-day week following an eight-week trial, during which time employees reported lower levels of stress, higher levels of job satisfaction and a greater sense of work-life balance. And despite the reduced hours, productivity did not decline. In fact, according to founder Andrew Barnes, the company is performing even better.

As Barnes told CNBC program *The Exchange*, '*This is all about working smarter, not working longer. We have this perception that you've got to work five days a week, 9-5. What we are really talking about is changing how people are behaving when they are at the office.*'

People can work fewer hours and increase output. I have experienced this firsthand. For example, my leadership training at one organisation focused on empowering others. Specifically, empowering them to work *on* the business rather than *in* it. When I applied this in another executive role over several years, I found I was only working half of the time that I had been initially. My team had improved its productivity, ironically with forty per cent fewer people, as it was doing more meaningful work for the business. This is a skill, rather than knowledge, that people can use.

A mentor once said to me that choosing the right things to do is often more difficult than doing everything. I have shared this philosophy with technology teams that I have led, emphasising the value of concentrating on one activity – and doing it well – rather than completing high volumes of work. Basically, my advice is to deliver the things of the greatest value sooner, rather than being distracted by a multitude of other things at the periphery.

Addressing digital burnout

'I feel burnout comes as a result of consistent over-simulation.'

– Dinesh Paliwal

David: The pressure to work longer hours is not the only challenge modern-day office workers face. In our always-on, always-connected world, an inability to 'switch off' – as in, not answering emails around the clock – is becoming an increasingly contentious issue.

In 2017, France introduced 'the right to disconnect', which requires companies with more than fifty employees to draw up a charter ensuring employees' rights to disconnect. France has a thirty-five-hour work week, which is one of the most regulated labour markets in the world. Specific companies have implemented similar policies. For example, Volkswagen prevents emails from being delivered to employees when they are off-shift or on holiday. Other companies – including Daimler, BMW, Allianz-France, telco Orange and IT company Atos – also have restrictions around employees' use of email.

In an interview with NBC News in 2017, the Managing Director of Reboot Online Marketing, Shai Aharony, said an email ban for employees on holiday did not last long as it wasn't practical. He said, '*So we relaxed the rules slightly and we put in this policy which encourages people to not send email, or to ask themselves the question whether this email that they're about to send out of working hours is actually urgent enough to be sent out, and that works perfectly.*'

A colleague at Microsoft in the UK, who had been working there for a considerable period, created an interesting out-of-office message when he went on holiday. It was something along the lines of: '*I am currently on vacation. I am not reading emails and I will be deleting them upon my return. If your email is important and requires a reply from me, please resend it when I return to the office on [date].*'

We all talked about it. However, nobody else was brave enough to do it.

According to Cary Cooper, a professor of psychology and health at the University of Manchester in the UK, in almost all developed countries, the leading cause of workplace absence is disorders like stress, anxiety and depression. He told NBC News, '*It used to be musculoskeletal – backache and things like that. It's also the leading cause of presenteeism – people going to work ill – so they're present at work, but they're not delivering any added value.*'

Digital burnout is a problem. In 2017, Cooper asked major employers what guidance they offer to employees to avoid this and discovered there was very little. Research indicates the continued blur in work/life balance is contributing to unprecedented levels of poor mental health. In fact, having the resources to work 24/7 has been shown to increase the risk of burnout. COVID-19 has only exacerbated this. According to a survey by FlexJobs and Mental Health America, seventy-five per cent of the workers surveyed have experienced burnout – and forty per cent said it was a direct result of the pandemic. Now more than ever, businesses need to ensure they create a workplace environment that nurtures employee mental health and wellbeing. This is an issue that will endure if not addressed.

The lure of the start-up

'Running a start-up is like eating glass. You just start to like the taste of your own blood.'

– Sean Parker

David: One of the ways in which younger people are attempting to achieve greater work/life balance – and perhaps take more control of their career – is by launching their own business. But is this the right approach? I did not start my business until I was well into my forties. I thought I was very late. Yet, according to research conducted by MIT Sloan School of Management, which analysed 2.7 million people who founded companies between 2007 and 2014, the average age of entrepreneurs who started a company (which went on to hire just one employee) was forty-two. Meanwhile, the average age of founders who started a high-growth company was forty-five.

The wisdom and experience of a middle-aged start-up founder almost certainly contributes to the start-up's success. Yet, increasingly, start-up founders are aged in their twenties and thirties. In some cases, the seed is planted before they have even graduated from university. According to one US university professor, a decade after wanting to work for the likes of Goldman Sachs, IBM and Unilever, it was Google, Facebook, Apple and Amazon who became the next big draw as employers, but now students want to do their own thing.

In a 2018 *Business Insider* article, Tomas Chamorro-Premuzic, who has been teaching MBA students for more than fifteen years, said, *'Now, the vast majority tell me, "You know, I'm going to be a start-up guy. I'm launching something. I'm going to create the next big X, Y, Z." Who are we to crush their spirits? But I think we have a responsibility to inform people that the probability of attaining that is really, really, really low, and that to actually attain it, they're going* [to] *have to sacrifice so many things.'*

The article highlights the rise of 'entrepreneurship porn', which is *'luring many ambitious young Americans into launching their own companies when they might be better off joining a more established organisation.'*

According to 2017 data from the US Bureau of Labor Statistics, only about twenty per cent of new businesses survive longer than a year. Often, those who fail in business go on to fail again and again, only seeking paid employment as a last resort. I have met some of these people when I have recruited for organisations. Their experiences are interesting but not necessarily relevant in a regular job, and the human resources team will often question whether they are a good 'fit' for the company.

They may have been a managing director, working for themselves from their kitchen table, but do they truly have the skills of a managing director – or did they simply assign themselves this title? A proven entrepreneur once said to me that launching a start-up is like starting a band. Lots of people flirt with the idea, but how many are truly committed – and have the necessary skills to succeed?

Despite claims to the contrary, a start-up cannot succeed on passion alone. In fact, passion can become your peril, says Noah Wasserman, author of *The Founder's Dilemmas: Anticipating and Avoiding the Pitfalls That Can Sink a Startup.* According to

Wasserman, passion can mislead you into thinking you are readier to start a company than you really are.

Other ways to approach entrepreneurship

'Entrepreneurship is not only about starting businesses but is an attitude to life.'

– Matt Hancock

Michelle: Another potential contributor to the rise of 'entrepreneurship porn' is the idea of entrepreneurship as a status symbol. This is highlighted in the Global Entrepreneurship Monitor (GEM) 2018/2019 Global Report, which profiles forty-nine economies. The report states:

> *'...most European and North American countries show lower levels of attitudes about entrepreneurship as a career choice than about the status of entrepreneurs, illustrating how more people hold entrepreneurs in high regard than believe this is something they or others should venture into.'*

The report also shows whether people believe it is easy to start a business in their home country – and whether there is a correlation between ease of starting a business and attitudes towards entrepreneurship. In this regard, Sweden came up as an interesting example because, even though three-quarters of Swedish adults think it's easy to start a business, less than half think it's a good career choice. According to the report, *'This illustrates that there may be more viable career alternatives, such as becoming an entrepreneurial employee.'*

The report defines entrepreneurial employee activity as entrepreneurship among employees of existing organisations. This includes developing or launching new goods or services, or setting up a new business unit, a new establishment or a subsidiary. According to the report, entrepreneurial employee activity is most prevalent in Europe. In fact, in Sweden, Germany and Cyprus, entrepreneurship is at least as likely to occur in organisations as it is in independent start-ups.

The report encourages other countries to follow suit, providing it fits with prevailing societal norms and values:

> *'For example, encouraging more people to start businesses in a society that is heavily risk-averse may be less promising than stimulating entrepreneurial employee behaviour. For the latter, cooperation with employers is essential. In this case, rather than focusing on new regulations, the challenge lies in creating organisational environments that reward creativity and proactive behaviour.'*

I cannot say I was ever an entrepreneurial employee. But for at least a year, I was what is known as a chicken entrepreneur. This is someone who keeps their day job while building their business on the side. Granted, there is nothing overly 'sexy' about this style of entrepreneurship. Chipping away at a side hustle does not have the same wow factor as 'I quit my job and used my life savings to launch my business.' But it did allow me to grow my client base slowly but steadily, ensuring that when I finally took the plunge and went out on my own, I had much more to draw on than that special blend of passion and Gen Y optimism.

The Law of Jante

*'The first step toward change is awareness.
The second step is acceptance.'*

– **Nathaniel Branden**

David: When we started researching for this book, I told Michelle about my time at Microsoft and working with colleagues across Europe. I particularly enjoyed working with the Scandinavians; there was a high level of trust, people were honest about what was possible, and it was rewarding. The Scandinavians have an approach to life and work known as 'Janteloven'. Janteloven, which translates to 'the Law of Jante' in English, is a well-known term in Scandinavian countries. Scandinavia Standard (a website that describes itself as 'your one-stop destination for Scandinavian lifestyle'), states:

> *'Janteloven's social code dictates emphasis on collective accomplishments and well-being, and disdains focus on individual achievements. It is an underlying Scandinavian philosophy principle that applies across Denmark, Norway, Sweden, Finland, and Iceland. Understanding Janteloven is paramount to understanding both the history and modern-day cultures of these countries.'*

The term was originally coined by the Danish-Norwegian author Aksel Sandemose. In his 1933 novel *A Fugitive Crosses His Tracks*, he created ten rules that define Janteloven. In essence, the rules state that individuals shouldn't think of themselves as better than the community as a whole.

Here is the full list:

1. You're not to think you are anything special.
2. You're not to think you are as good as we are.

3. You're not to think you are smarter than we are.
4. You're not to imagine yourself better than we are.
5. You're not to think you know more than we do.
6. You're not to think you are more important than we are.
7. You're not to think you are good at anything.
8. You're not to laugh at us.
9. You're not to think anyone cares about you.
10. You're not to think you can teach us anything.

Now, while the rules may seem a bit oppressive, they bring a light-heartedness to the lives of Scandinavians. This is seen in a Carlsberg beer commercial featuring Danish actor Mads Mikkelsen (Google his name and you are sure to recognise his face). In the ad, Mikkelsen clumsily but happily rides a bike through the streets of Copenhagen. Despite being dressed in a nice suit, he has a series of mishaps, but continues unfazed. There is a level of pride mixed with humility, which endears to you the Scandinavian way.

Based on my experience, Scandinavians are stylish and committed, but do not take themselves too seriously, with an exceptional commitment to their broader environment and community. So, how does Janteloven translate to the workplace?

Instead of prioritising personal success, it emphasises adherence to – and support of – the collective. As an example, during COVID-19, Princess Sofia of Sweden volunteered at a local hospital, completing a rigorous online training program to assist nurses on the frontline. Sofia helped doctors and nurses with housekeeping tasks, including working in the kitchen, disinfecting medical equipment and cleaning up. Despite her 'status' as a royal, Sofia was very much an equal, working alongside her fellow Swedes and happy to do menial tasks.

In an interview with TNW, American tech executive Philip Hanson discussed what it was like to move from the United States to Copenhagen. He said he quickly noticed Denmark's advanced work culture, which is built on a strong foundation of trust and a true sense of equality. It is not uncommon to see a CEO cleaning coffee cups, for example. He cited this as an indication of the high level of mutual respect between colleagues, regardless of their 'status' within the organisation.

And he brought it back to Janteloven, stating, '*When you work in that way it informs a level of trust, which is one of the great things of working here in Denmark. People trust that you are doing your job well and you can trust that when you receive feedback that the person means it.*'

Rather than having to 'earn' trust, employees are trusted from the outset. This helps prevent misunderstandings and minimises unnecessary office politics. Phillip said the 'you say what you mean, and you mean what you say' attitude could benefit American companies too. I suspect it would be of benefit to everyone, everywhere.

I have worked across half a dozen industries in my career, some with very little politics and others with a considerable amount. Based on these experiences, the consequences of politics are not truly understood until something goes wrong. In those workplace environments where there is minimal politics, there is a greater level of support for one another. When things have not gone to plan, I have seen people take accountability for something they were not involved in and own it. In highly political environments, I have seen people distance themselves from something they were involved in and create a blame narrative. An obsession with individuality and personal success – and the need to be 'better' than one's peers – could be contributing to this.

A cautionary tale about hierarchy

'I would say the hierarchy has made terrible errors in judgement and it has to seek forgiveness by its members.'

– William P. Leahy

David: Sweden is often ranked as one of the world's best countries, across a range of different metrics. But there is a story about a historic Swedish ship that I'd like to share with you. It serves as a cautionary tale about the dangers of 'status' and hierarchy, which are worth remembering in the context of the workplace.

In Stockholm, there is a wonderful, reclaimed warship called the Vasa. Built between 1626 and 1628, the ship was 157 feet long and featured sixty-four customised, bronze cannons. Unfortunately, after sailing just 1,300 metres on her maiden voyage (on August 10, 1628), the ship sank. Amazingly, some 333 years later, in 1961, it was recovered and found to be in exceptional condition, due to the temperature of the water.

So, what caused the ship to sink in the first place?

The Vasa was ornately decorated to represent the power and glory of Gustavus Adolphus, a Swedish king who began ruling as a teenager and led Sweden through one of the most turbulent periods in the country's history. King Adolphus is known for turning the tide of the Thirty Years War and for saving Protestantism in Germany from annihilation.

He ordered the building of the Vasa to assist the Swedish naval forces. Prior to its maiden voyage, engineers inspected the Vasa and discovered a flaw. The upper structure of the hull was too heavy due to the weight of the cannons and ornaments. The engineers informed the officials in the Swedish court, who were too afraid to inform the king of this flaw. When the ship commenced its maiden voyage, the hull quickly filled with water due to strong winds and waves, causing the ship to sink.

The ship now sits in the Vasa Museum in Stockholm. The Vasa is the world's best-preserved 17th-century ship, and the Vasa Museum is the most visited museum in Scandinavia. I saw the ship with a colleague when I visited Stockholm. The sheer scale of it is frightening. And it made me wonder: If the Law of Jante had existed back then, would the outcome have been different? Would the engineers and court officials have shared their concerns with King Adolphus? If they had, perhaps the ship's flaws would've been fixed, and the ship wouldn't have sunk. Let this serve as a cautionary tale about the dangers of status and hierarchy, particularly in a working environment.

Psychological safety in the workplace

'Safety is something that happens between your ears, not something you hold in your hands.'

– Jeff Cooper

Michelle: I think the story of the Vasa also highlights the importance of psychological safety in the workplace. This is a term I first came across in relation to Google. Over a two-year period, Google set out to discover what makes an effective team. The research team identified 180 teams to study – 115 project teams in engineering and sixty-five pods in sales, with a mix of high- and low-performing teams. The study tested how both team composition (personality traits, skills and so on) and team dynamics (what it was like to work with teammates) impact team effectiveness.

The researchers measured team effectiveness in four different ways:

1. Executive evaluation of the team
2. Team leader evaluation of the team
3. Team member evaluation of the team
4. Sales performance against quarterly quota

The researchers found that what really mattered was less about who was on the team, and more about how the team worked together. With regard to the latter, they identified five key factors:

- **Psychological safety:** Team members feel safe to take risks and be vulnerable in front of each other.
- **Dependability:** Team members get things done on time and meet the company's expectations or standards.
- **Structure and clarity:** Team members have clear roles, plans and goals.
- **Meaning:** Work is personally important to team members.
- **Impact:** Team members think their work matters and creates change.

Of these five, psychological safety was identified as by far the most important. Google states:

'Psychological safety refers to an individual's perception of the consequences of taking an interpersonal risk or a belief that the team is safe for risk taking in the face of being seen as ignorant, incompetent, negative, or disruptive. In a team with high psychological safety, teammates feel safe to take risks around their team members. They feel confident that no one on the team will embarrass or punish anyone else for admitting a mistake, asking a question, or offering a new idea.'

According to Google, the construct of 'team psychological safety' was first introduced by Harvard professor Amy Edmondson. To measure a team's level of psychological safety, Edmondson asked team members how strongly they agreed or disagreed with these statements:

1. If you make a mistake on this team, it is often held against you.
2. Members of this team can bring up problems and tough issues.
3. People on this team sometimes reject others for being different.
4. It is safe to take a risk on this team.
5. It is difficult to ask other members of this team for help.
6. No one on this team would deliberately act in a way that undermines my efforts.
7. Working with members of this team, my unique skills and talents are valued and utilised.

To return to the example of the Vasa, I would say there was a complete lack of psychological safety among the engineers and court officials. A directive came from the king and it had to be followed – regardless of how flawed it was, or the consequences. Scarily, this is still happening in workplaces around the world. It could be something as simple as being too afraid to clarify the goal of a particular project, for fear of sounding incompetent.

In a TEDx Talk, Amy Edmondson suggests three ways to foster team psychological safety:

1. Frame the work as a learning problem, not an execution problem.
2. Acknowledge your own shortcomings.
3. Model curiosity and ask lots of questions.

These are simple things you can do, as an individual, to facilitate psychological safety in the workplace, particularly in your immediate team.

On another note, I think the overly ornate style of the Vasa also highlights the perils of our obsession with appearances, which stems from an innate desire to impress others and 'be the best'. It is ironic that the weight of the cannons and ornaments was ultimately the ship's undoing. There's merit in humility!

Reflection

David: We started this chapter with a discussion on globalisation, which has resulted in various benefits as well as problems. One problem is excessive work hours and the subsequent rise of workplace burnout. In response to this, some organisations are introducing shorter working weeks. Workers are also seeking alternatives, such as starting their own business. Research indicates the most successful founders are in their forties, although the chicken entrepreneurship movement is popular with people who wish to remain employed while starting a side hustle. We also touched on some lesser-known ideas, such as the Scandinavian concept of Janteloven (which is a focus on collective accomplishments and wellbeing, thus taking the onus off the individual) and the importance of psychological safety in the workplace.

When reflecting on this chapter, consider:

- Do you think globalisation is ultimately better or worse for the planet and the human race?
- What global trends are impacting your industry?
- What are your thoughts on 'death by overwork'?
- Have you experienced digital burnout? If so, how did you address it?

- Would you ever consider launching a start-up or working for yourself? Why or why not?
- Do you agree with the concept of Janteloven? Why or why not?
- What is the level of psychological safety in your business or the organisation you work for? How does this affect you?
- As a society, where should we place our focus to prepare future generations for the workplace?

CHAPTER 4

Australians at Work

*'In terms of being Australian, I think
a big part of it is the determination to
prove yourself, just like Aussie actors.'*

– Keiynan Lonsdale

Michelle: In this chapter, which focuses specifically on Australian workers and organisations, I start things off with a simple question: How digital are we really? I then highlight the rise of the gig economy, as well as some of the challenges that come with working from home. Meanwhile, David touches on some of the complexities regarding the management of contractors. We then turn our focus to the specific challenges facing men and women in the workplace. These include the link between men's work and wellbeing, and some of the disparities and obstacles women grapple with, particularly once they begin that delicate juggle of work and motherhood.

How digital are we really?

*'We live in a digital world, but we're
fairly analogue creatures.'*

– Omar Ahmad

Michelle: You may (not) be surprised to learn that most Australian and New Zealand businesses are lagging when it comes to digital business progress. This is according to the Gartner 2019 CIO Agenda Survey, which gathered data from more than 3,000 CIOs in eighty-nine countries and across all major industries, including 161 respondents from Australia and New Zealand (ANZ).

The survey shows just thirty per cent of ANZ organisations are starting to scale and harvest value from their digital investments. Meanwhile, the remaining seventy per cent are still evolving their digital business foundations. The survey results indicate that flat IT budget growth is hindering digital transformation. In 2019, IT budgets grew by just 1.5 per cent among ANZ businesses, compared with an expected growth rate of 2.9 per cent among CIOs globally.

In a company press release, Brian Ferreira, vice president of executive programs at Gartner, said, '*The risk during these uncertain times with limited budgets is to make short-term investment decisions, which can slow or even reverse digital business transformation progress. For those who stick to their plans and focus on the long-term vision, the returns will be there.*'

This is yet another case of Australian short-termism. If Australian businesses want to survive and compete in a global marketplace, they need to get serious about digital investment and strategies. This is echoed in a 2018 government report. The Industry Insights report, titled 'Future productivity', asks: How digital are Australian industries? The answer is: Despite the potential benefits of digital technologies, the rate of adoption is uneven.

According to the Office of the Chief Economist, digital technologies could boost the economy by $140–250 *billion* by 2025. However, adoption varies widely across industries. For example, finance firms use cloud computing at three times the rate of agriculture. The report states:

'Businesses across all industries have a significant way to go in adopting technology to realise the full potential these technologies can bring. Adoption of digital technology is key to Australia's international competitiveness. Australia currently ranks 13 out of 63 countries in the Institute for Management Development digital competitiveness ranking, lagging behind countries such as the US, Canada and Singapore.

'Digital uptake will be critical to addressing slow productivity. Uptake is also key to global competitiveness in traditional industries like mining and advanced manufacturing as well as emerging priorities in services industries....New technologies transform cost structures, enable the creation of new business models and methods of production, and bring entirely new products and services to market...Productivity growth will be improved with broader adoption across all industries.'

Rise of the gig economy

'Independent contractors – a rapidly growing piece of the workforce – can often achieve the best quality of life. They can choose from where they work, whom they work for and for how long.'

– Maynard Webb

Michelle: By 2023, one-third of the workforce is expected to be contractors. That is according to an annual study conducted in June 2018 by recruitment company Robert Half. The research polled 3,840 business leaders in twelve countries, including Australia.

The research reveals that business leaders aim to achieve a 66:34 split between permanent and temporary workers by 2023. This highlights the incredible rise of the professional gig economy, which is completely transforming the way people work.

Gig workers are independent contractors, online platform workers, contract firm workers, on-call workers and temporary workers. Typically, they provide their services on an on-demand basis. And it seems employers are increasingly drawn to these types of workers; the Robert Half research found ninety-seven per cent of business leaders identified benefits of adopting a more flexible approach to recruitment. These include more control over staffing and recruitment costs (identified by thirty-six per cent of the business leaders surveyed), support for long-term absences, such as parental leave, secondments or sick leave (thirty-four per cent), and better management of workload fluctuations (thirty-two per cent).

According to the Australian Bureau of Statistics, more than one million Australians are classified as independent contractors. Robert Half reveals Australian hiring managers predict a 70:30 split between permanent and temporary employees by 2023.

A separate survey, designed to support a Victorian government inquiry into the on-demand workforce, further highlights the burgeoning nature of Australia's gig economy. The survey of more than 14,000 people – jointly conducted by Queensland University of Technology, the University of Adelaide and the University of Technology Sydney – is Australia's largest ever published survey regarding the on-demand economy.

Here are some of the findings:

- 7.1 per cent of respondents use a digital platform for work or have done so in the past twelve months.
- 15.5 per cent of platform workers consider gig work 'essential for meeting their basic needs', while 24.3 per

cent regard it as an 'important part of overall income, but not essential'.

- The most common digital platform workers include men aged eighteen to thirty-four, students, temporary residents, people with a disability and those who do not speak English at home.
- Women are half as likely as men to work on digital platforms.
- Platform workers report high satisfaction with the flexibility of gig work but are less satisfied with their incomes.
- The five most common platforms used by Australian workers are Airtasker (34.8 per cent), Uber (22.7 per cent), Freelancer (11.8 per cent), Uber Eats (10.8 per cent) and Deliveroo (8.2 per cent).

As a freelancer myself, I have never used a digital platform to find work. However, my husband found our chartered accountant, James, on Airtasker in 2017. James had recently started his own business and was looking to build his client base. He not only handles our tax returns but oversees our self-managed super fund too. It is worth noting that my husband also has an accounting degree, so he's exceptionally picky about whom he works with. To this day, my husband remains a happy and loyal client of James, often referring him to our friends and family.

In my experience, the gig economy naturally lends itself to B2C (business-to-customer) working relationships, such as the relationship my husband and I have formed with our accountant. However, as David explains in the following section, it seems B2B (business-to-business) working relationships are more complex where gig or contract workers are involved.

The complex nature of managing contractors

'The powers that technology and independent contracting give to workers enables them to take greater control of their careers to preserve work-life balance.'

– Elise Stefanik

David: With the onset of the gig economy, organisations can hire gun specialists for a specific task within a set time frame. Upon completion of the task, the gig worker, or contractor, moves on.

When I established my business, I recruited several contractors – all of whom worked remotely.

My company logos were awarded to a graphic designer in Eastern Europe; I have never actually spoken with this person. The illustrations for my first book and this book were completed by two different people in Asia. Further, I eventually met the co-author of this book, Michelle, in person due to a client commitment in her home city. Before this, I had engaged her for a post-publish editing task in relation to my first book, despite having never met her.

But in a more traditional working environment, I have seen some of the drawbacks of hiring and working with contractors. If the relationship is not managed appropriately, it can be damaging – for everyone involved. Contractors will work alongside your permanent employees; in many ways, they are indistinguishable from them. However, the way they are treated and rewarded can have a significant impact on an organisation's culture.

In a 2019 *Forbes* article, Marissa Geist, COO of Cielo (which helps companies attract and hire talent), said that while it might make sense to hire a contractor for short-term projects or to save money, it may ultimately prove unwise. She went on to say:

> *'At the end of the day, there is no substitute for engaged, effective, long-term talent. Despite the potential cost savings that a contractor can provide, if you fail to make contractors feel engaged and connected to your company, the drag on culture and momentum can actually be more costly than the immediate savings that contractors bring in the short term.'*

Google has encountered these very challenges. At one point, it got so bad that a group of Google employees protested, demanding higher pay and better benefits for the company's contract workers. The group accused Google of having a *'two-tier system'*, which *'treats some workers as expendable'*.

As the gig economy continues to grow, organisations need to revisit and, if necessary, evolve their approach to hiring and managing contractors to ensure the health of *all* their staff and, in turn, the health of their business. I see this as a vast area of opportunity to access global talent, potentially boosting the contribution of organisations' locally employed talent.

Working from home is a double-edged sword

> *'When I started working from home, I made a promise to myself to go out at least once a day.'*
>
> – Jane Fallon

Michelle: Prior to COVID-19, when I told people I worked from home, one of the things they would often say was, 'Oh, you're so lucky – no commute!' It is true. I don't have to stand on a crowded train or sit in bumper-to-bumper traffic on the freeway. And for that, I am incredibly grateful – especially when you consider the lengthy commute times of my fellow taxpayers.

According to a 2019 Household, Income and Labour Dynamics in Australia (HILDA) Survey, Australian city workers' average commute has blown out to sixty-six minutes a day. The survey, which is based on interviews with about 17,000 Australians, reveals that in 2002, workers averaged 3.7 hours' commuting time per week. By 2017, this had jumped to 4.5 hours.

In 2017, workers in the state's five major capitals (Sydney, Melbourne, Brisbane, Adelaide and Perth) spent more than an hour travelling to and from work each day. The average commute was about sixty-six minutes, up from around fifty-five minutes since 2002. Across the country, average daily commuting times increased from around forty-nine minutes in 2002 to almost one hour in 2017.

According to the survey, long-distance commuters are less likely to be satisfied with their working hours, work-life balance and even their pay packet. They are also less productive and engaged, and more likely to suffer physical and mental strain.

For many people, COVID-19 has changed the way they work – possibly forever. This is highlighted in a BBC Worklife article, which states, *'For those who can work from home...our daily experience of work will change significantly. Commuters will gain an hour back on average in their day and estimates suggest that post pandemic, some portion of the week will involve working from home – from one to three days a week.'*

In my experience, working from home is a double-edged sword. Sure, there is no commute. And many workers enjoy the added autonomy and find they are *more* productive at home than in the office.

However, remote workers face their own set of struggles, including an inability to switch off from work, loneliness, and difficulties collaborating or communicating with others. These struggles, and others, are reflected in the following diagram, which is part of the 2020 State of Remote Work Report, produced by social media manager Buffer. The report is based on a survey of over 3,500 remote workers in different countries, including Australia.

What's your biggest struggle with working remotely?

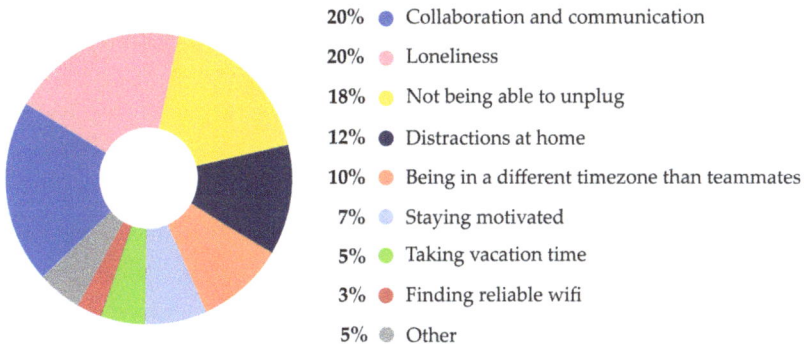

20% ●	Collaboration and communication
20% ●	Loneliness
18% ●	Not being able to unplug
12% ●	Distractions at home
10% ●	Being in a different timezone than teammates
7% ●	Staying motivated
5% ●	Taking vacation time
3% ●	Finding reliable wifi
5% ●	Other

Source: 2020 State of Remote Work report

These struggles became more evident during the pandemic, when millions of workers around the world were suddenly required to work from home. For many people, it proved to be a real challenge – one they simply were not prepared for. I know many of my own colleagues and friends were keen to return to their offices once restrictions eased.

For the most part, I love working from home. I love working in my pyjamas for an hour or two, although I always get dressed eventually. I love being able to duck out for a coffee catch-up or run errands. Most of all, I love being able to work from anywhere. My husband and I even lived in Thailand for a while, taking advantage of the digital nomad lifestyle.

But I struggle to switch off from work. After all, my laptop is *just there*...I can fire it up at any time of the day or night. And yes, it can be incredibly lonely. Sometimes, I would love nothing more than to wander into a staff kitchen and have a chat with a co-worker.

In the wake of COVID-19, many companies have indicated they will continue to facilitate remote working to some extent. However, companies need to ensure remote workers receive support – not only in a practical sense (like leadership and tech support) but with regard to their health and wellbeing too. Companies like KPMG are already putting in place measures to boost connection among remote workers, including:

- Starting online meetings with five minutes of non-work-related chatter, whereby participants can share personal anecdotes and/or ask each other questions.
- Creating virtual communities based on shared interests or 'neighbourhoods', where staff live in the same area, to help build a sense of connection.
- Establishing buddy systems to provide one-on-one connections between two people.

I look forward to seeing what other companies come up with. But I also believe individuals need to reach out if they are struggling – either to their employer or to a support service such as Beyond Blue.

The link between men's work and wellbeing

'Men cannot live by exchanging articles, but producing them. They live by work not trade.'

– John Ruskin

David: In Australia, deaths as a result of suicide occur among men at a rate more than three times greater than for women. This is a deeply concerning trend, which is fuelled by a range of different things. However, one of the less documented factors is the link between men and their work, and the impact this can have on their psychological wellbeing.

In an article for the *Washington Examiner,* Suzanne Venker reports on the death of former Obama adviser Alan Kreuger, who took his own life in 2019. Prior to his death, Krueger, who was a labour economist, researched the link between low labour force participation and opioid addiction. According to his research, prime-age men who are unemployed *'experience notably low levels of emotional wellbeing throughout their days'* and *'derive relatively little meaning from their daily activities'.*

Venker states:

> *'So what is the link between men, work, and their psychological well-being? That work is at the core of their identity....For men, their ability to provide for their families is how they gain a sense of purpose. Thus, a man who is stripped of his ability to earn...doesn't feel like a man at all. He becomes rudderless. He feels useless....We may not like that men need employment in a unique and primal way, but we can't will it away, nor should we try.'*

Venker identifies other things that have demoted men, including anti-male propaganda in the media and universities, and commercials that make men, and dads in particular, look silly. As a white, middle-aged man, I have observed men quietly hurting, as jobs have been lost, marriages broken up and dreams shattered. But rather than voice their struggles, men often go quiet, as they do not really know how to discuss their feelings – or simply don't want to. This is part of the problem.

'We tell boys that "boys don't cry",' Colman Driscoll, a former Lifeline executive, told BBC Future in 2019. *'We condition boys from a very young age to not express emotion, because to express emotion is to be "weak".'*

As I wrote earlier, many men within my professional peer group have contacted me in the past two years – since I founded my business and wrote my first book. Often, these men are concerned about their professional future. They have observed policies that improve diversity within organisations (and rightfully so), but they are anxious. Many of them saw their career mapped out within a particular organisation, but their future role is now limited. They are not prepared for a future outside of a corporate environment.

Alan Krueger recognised the link between men's work and their health. In fact, he even issued a call to action, stating, *'Addressing the decades-long slide in labour force participation by prime-age men should be a national priority.'*

Within the workforce, I believe we need to balance the participation of prime-age men with diversity. They both need to be achieved in parallel. In Australia, there are already some initiatives to help men address their mental health, like R U OK? Day. Men also have access to Men's Sheds, which can be found in cities and towns across the country. The Men's Shed website states:

'Good health is based on many factors including feeling good about yourself, being productive, contributing to your community, connecting with friends and maintaining an active body and mind. Becoming a member of a Men's Shed provides a safe and busy environment where men can find many of these things in an atmosphere of old-fashioned mateship. And, importantly, there is no pressure. Men can just come and have a yarn and a cuppa if that is all they're looking for.'

The website also states that some Men's Sheds, via a management committee, enable men to work on community projects, specific Men's Shed projects or a project of their choice in their own time. In addition to these support services, if we know that a man's work is something they identify strongly with, perhaps there is an opportunity to initiate programs that help out-of-work men start their own businesses. Some men have been interested in how I transitioned into my own business; there were limited resources applicable to help me. I see this as an area of opportunity for me to help men in the future. After a couple of years in business, I may be able to write a book about it.

Women versus women

'We live in a society that wants to pit women against each other, and it's our job to resist the tyranny of that.'

– Lena Dunham

David: Early in the last decade of the last century, I began managing teams. Since then, I have managed a lot of teams across many industries, in various countries, and I have been surprised by stories from female colleagues who were frustrated with their female manager. Sometimes, I shared the same manager and had a great experience with them. Why was it different for women?

The private conversations with my female colleagues were very delicate, and I feel uncomfortable writing about them. These women felt a lack of understanding from their manager, and that any support offered was conditional. In some instances, the manager expected significant personal sacrifice. Sometimes, this manager did not have children and didn't understand the obligations of having children. If the manager did have children, there was often an expectation that someone else (perhaps a nanny or grandparent) would care for them.

These women felt judged and, in some instances, unfairly assessed. The judgement would sometimes extend to the length of time they had taken away from the workplace to care for their children. In some instances, the employment contract type (either full-time or part-time) also played a role, as women who worked part-time had their capability questioned.

If you think this is all just anecdotal, consider this: Research shows that when women have a preference as to the gender of their bosses and colleagues, it's largely for men. In a 2017 article for *The Atlantic*, Olga Khazan writes:

> 'A 2009 study published in the journal Gender in Management found, for example, that although women believe other women make good managers, "the female workers did not actually want to work for them." The longer a woman had been in the workforce, the less likely she was to want a female boss.

> 'In 2011, Kim Elsesser, a lecturer at UCLA, analysed responses from more than 60,000 people and found that women – even those who were managers themselves – were more likely to want a male boss than a female one.'

Why?

The same article goes on to reference Joyce Benenson, a psychologist at Emmanuel College in Boston. According to Benenson, women are evolutionarily predestined not to collaborate with women they are not related to. Her research indicates that females are:

- Less willing than males to cooperate with lower-status individuals of the same gender,
- More likely to dissolve same-gender friendships, and
- More willing to socially exclude one another.

Benenson believes that women undermine one another because they have always had to compete for mates and for resources for their offspring. According to Benenson, women *'can gather around smiling and laughing, exchanging polite, intimate, and even warm conversation, while simultaneously destroying one another's careers. The contrast is jarring.'*

The article also explores the idea of the 'queen bee' concept, whereby senior women cope with gender discrimination by emphasising how different they are from other women. Queen bees typically emerge *'when women are a marginalised group in the workplace, have made big sacrifices for their career, or are already predisposed to show little "gender identification" – camaraderie with other women.'*

As someone who was fortunate enough to manage a diverse team in the past, I find this disheartening, as the potential of a team is diminished if diversity is not encouraged and celebrated. The research clearly indicates the benefits of diversity, particularly in relation to women. In 2011, I joined the Male Champions of Change community in Australia, with a focus on improving gender diversity and remuneration. I am proud to have worked at several organisations – as an employee or as a service provider –

that truly believe in and action this. Also, as a father of three, two of whom are girls, I am optimistic about their future.

The distorted nature of female leadership

'In the future, there will be no female leaders. There will just be leaders.'

– Sheryl Sandberg

Michelle: I must be honest. To date, I have had better working relationships with male bosses than female bosses. But I certainly do not think that female managers are inherently more hostile or 'territorial' than male managers. I think some women in leadership roles (some, not all!) feel they have to assert themselves in a more mindful, proactive way than their male counterparts.

In my experience, male managers are more relaxed; they do not feel the need to 'back themselves' the way some female managers do. Some of the male head honchos I have worked for have come across as incredibly laidback – almost *too* laidback, in some cases. Would they be so laidback if they were female? I doubt it. I believe that if you are a woman in a leadership role, you're expected to act a certain way, partly to show that you 'deserve' the job.

It is also worth pointing out that *male* managers can be hostile towards their *male* staff. Right before my very eyes, I have seen male bosses go soft on female employees – and come down on male employees like a tonne of bricks. The difference is that when a male boss is demanding – and perhaps a little unforgiving – of his male staff, it is not labelled bullying. It is 'challenging' or 'motivating'. Perhaps female bosses are not any more aggressive than male bosses. Perhaps we simply cannot handle a female boss being aggressive in the first place.

According to an article in the *Harvard Business Review* (*HBR*), which looked at 200 performance reviews within one company, there does indeed appear to be a double standard. *HBR* tallied the number of references to being 'too aggressive' in the reviews. More than three-quarters (seventy-six per cent) of these instances were attributed to women.

According to Singaporean journalist Vivien Shiao, there's no easy solution to this – but an awareness of our double standards is a good start. In a 2016 article for *The Business Times*, she wrote, '*As more women aspire and attain positions of power, the rest of the workforce must give them the support that they need, and this includes other women. Not only will this enable them to be more effective leaders, it also paves the way for other women.*'

Mothers in the workplace: A catch-22

*'The phrase "working mum"
makes me nervous.'*

– Victoria Coren Mitchell

David: The challenges for women extend far beyond the workplace. Professional women have also shared with me their exhaustion and guilt. Many are caring for ageing parents and/or young children, running a household and trying to build their career. All are grateful for their foremothers, who have championed equality. They feel a deep obligation to their daughters, nieces and other female family members to ensure these opportunities are maintained and enhanced. However, in some cases, their exhaustion has led to a range of other challenges.

For example, research indicates that while only two per cent of working women plan to leave the workforce for family reasons, forty-three per cent of highly qualified women opt out or off-ramp on their way back to work after starting a family. Having worked with colleagues all over the world, I have always struggled with the disparities of maternity leave periods. In the US, for example, a former colleague explained to me that she needed to return to her job just sixteen weeks after her baby's birth. In contrast, here in Australia and in the UK, my wife was able to take a full year off work following the birth of each of our children.

Today's professional career is dramatically different from what it was ten to fifteen years ago, as working mothers are connected to the office via technology. To have it all, they must be available to all. Some mothers agree to flexible hours with their employer, yet end up replying to emails at all hours.

The expectations we place on women, in addition to the pressure they put on themselves, is incredibly damaging. According to research published in the *Journal of Experimental Social Psychology* in 2017, when it comes to maternity leave, a woman is '*damned if she does and damned if she doesn't*'. The study – which included nearly 200 working men and women – found that women are viewed less favourably when they have a baby, whether they take maternity leave or not. Alarmingly, opinions did not differ based on age, nationality or parental status.

According to the research paper, it is '*imperative to introduce policies that enable parents to reconcile family and work demands... [but] we should be cognisant that the availability of these policies can inadvertently bring pressures of their own.*'

Madeline Heilman, one of the study's co-authors and a professor of psychology at New York University, said while society must work harder to fight these stereotypes, the burden does, unfortunately, fall on women to counteract them as best they can.

Her suggestions included speaking frankly to co-workers, staying in touch while on leave, and being mindful of how time is divided between home and the office.

Heilman said, '*I do a lot of research on gender stereotyping, and I wish I had better solutions. But the said truth is, women are really between a rock and a hard place when making this decision...it seems unlikely that working mothers will escape this dilemma any time soon.*'

The impossibility of being a Gen Y working mum

'You just keep going and keep going, and you sort of do the impossible.'

– Tina Fey

Michelle: I am deeply concerned about the insane pressure facing working mums, particularly those of my generation. According to Mary Beth Ferrante – a Gen Y mum-of-two and an advocate for creating inclusive workplaces for parents – millennial mothers feel overwhelmed and unsupported during the transition from motherhood to working mother.

In a 2018 *Forbes* article, she writes:

'No previous generation has applied more effort in creating a harmonious co-existence between work and life. For Baby Boomers and Gen X, it was normal to draw a line in the sand and expect family life and work to be separate. But with technology significantly changing the way we work today

and into the future, it is increasingly difficult to separate the two.

'Our ability, and now expectation, to respond to emails late into the evenings and weekends, has us wondering why flexible hours are still something to negotiate, or why we feel judged when we leave the office at 5pm to pick up our children, even though we are often getting to work hours earlier than others.'

Many of my friends are contending with the delicate – and, at times, seemingly impossible – task of balancing motherhood and work, particularly as the lines between work and home life continue to blur (thanks in part to technology, as Ferrante points out). The struggle is real, regardless of the type of work they do, what their partner does, how many children they have and how much help they have on hand.

Among all the millennial working mums I know – even the ones who work remotely – the biggest stress outside of motherhood itself is how to have some semblance of a career or simply earn money in a way that works for them and their family. This is something I'll discuss in more detail in Chapter 8.

Reflection

David: This chapter began with a question: How digital are we really? Research suggests Australian businesses have a long way to go in terms of digital competitiveness. However, a third of the Australian workforce is expected to be employed by the gig economy by 2023. The employment of contractors is not without complexity, however, nor is the increase in WFH (working from home). Looking at men and women in the workplace, we highlighted a number of ongoing challenges. The question is: Can these challenges be addressed – and how?

When reflecting on this chapter, consider:

- Do you agree that Australian businesses are lagging when it comes to digital business progress? What is your experience of this in your own business or the organisation you work for?
- How could Australian businesses improve their digital competitiveness?
- What are your thoughts on the gig economy and the growing number of contractors in the workforce? How does this affect you, either as a worker or an employer?
- How flexible is your business or organisation in terms of evolving its approach to remote working?
- What are your thoughts on the link between men's work and wellbeing? Have you experienced this yourself, or witnessed it in any men you know?
- How can we support men who lose their employment to create and launch their own businesses?
- What do you think of the notion of 'women versus women' in the workplace? Have you experienced this yourself, or witnessed it?
- How might we better support women in the workplace, particularly female leaders and working mothers?

PART 3

COMMUNITY

CHAPTER 5

The Human Struggle

*'We cannot live only for ourselves. A thousand
fibres connect us with our fellow men.'*

– Herman Melville

Michelle: In this chapter, David and I turn our focus to community. The Oxford Dictionary defines community as *'a group of people living in the same place or having a particular characteristic in common.'* We believe every human being should feel a sense of community. But what happens when communities begin to break down? In this chapter, we highlight some of the biggest challenges facing different communities throughout the world, including depression, prescription drug addiction and suicide. We also explore ways to help address these challenges, drawing on research as well as our own experiences.

The sad state of mental health in our global community

*'Mental health needs a great deal of
attention. It's the final taboo and it
needs to be faced and dealt with.'*

– Adam Ant

David: According to the World Health Organisation, suicide rates have increased by sixty per cent worldwide in the last forty-five years. Suicide is now among the three leading causes of death among those aged fifteen to forty-four. These figures do not include suicide attempts, which are up to twenty times more frequent than completed suicides. Traditionally, suicide rates were the highest among elderly males. However, rates among young people have been increasing; this group is now the highest at risk in a third of all countries. More than half (fifty-five per cent) of people who die by suicide are aged fifteen to forty-four, while forty-five per cent are aged forty-five and over.

In the US, males are four times more likely to die from suicide than females. Research indicates that suicide rates appear to be increasing within native and indigenous populations, such as Native Americans and indigenous Australians. Suicide rates within migrant communities, such as African and East Asian Americans or the black British community, are also becoming increasingly concerning.

According to the World Health Organisation (WHO), more than ninety per cent of suicides are associated with mental health disorders, particularly depression and substance abuse. The WHO states, 'Strategies involving restriction of access to common methods of suicide have proved to be effective in reducing suicide rates; however, there is a need to adopt multi-sectoral approaches involving other levels of intervention and activities, such as crisis centres.'

The WHO goes on to state that the prevention and treatment of depression, as well as alcohol and substance abuse, can reduce suicide rates. And among young people, school-based interventions – involving crisis management, self-esteem enhancement, and the development of coping skills and decision making – have been demonstrated to reduce the risk of suicide.

Suicide is not something that is openly discussed and, when it occurs, it leaves so many unanswered questions. What is alarming is the increasing rate of mental health issues among young people; it creates a sickening pit in my stomach. Some may have a view that the stigma surrounding mental health is reducing, which is leading to an increase in reporting. However, sadly, we are also seeing an increase in suicides and it is evident that we have a growing issue in our communities. If this trend continues, are we to see a substantial increase in suicide rates among future generations?

Prescription drugs: A growing epidemic

'America is one of few advanced nations that allow direct advertising of prescription drugs.'

– Robert Reich

David: In the context of mental health, it would be remiss of me not to discuss the impact of prescription drug use, which is ravaging certain countries. It is important to note that Michelle and myself are not medical professionals; this section of the book is based on our research and some personal anecdotes. We have both had experiences in our lives where people have become dependent on prescription medication.

During my professional career, I have led teams consisting of hundreds of people. I have probably managed between 4,000 and 5,000 people, and I have also participated in various employee representative groups. Some of my former colleagues had complicated medical issues that required support. In several instances, some struggled immensely with the withdrawal from antidepressants.

I did not realise the extent of the problem until I began researching it several years ago, after several people opened up to me about their struggles. After writing this section of the book over several days, I remain exceptionally concerned for those who are impacted by mental illness, particularly those taking antidepressants, and believe that pharmaceutical companies must be held more accountable for the overall impact of their drugs on users, including withdrawal.

In 2018, more than 67,000 Americans died from drug-involved overdose, including illicit drugs and prescription opioids, according to the Centers for Disease Control and Prevention (CDC). Synthetic narcotics or opioids were the main driver of drug overdose deaths, with a nearly twelvefold increase from 2012 to 2018.

According to DrugRehab.com, prescription drugs are now the most abused substances in the world behind alcohol and marijuana. Sadly, many users become addicted to prescription drugs while treating legitimate medical conditions such as pain or mental health problems. The website states:

> 'The amount of prescription opioids sold in the United States has nearly quadrupled since 1999, according to the CDC. The amount of pain Americans reported from 1999 to 2014 remained stable, yet the number of deaths from prescription opioids increased nearly fourfold during this time.'

Those suffering from addiction often struggle with cross-addictions too. In other words, they may be dependent on multiple substances – particularly as prescription drugs are expensive. According to the website, many opioid users turn to heroin as a cheaper alternative.

And if you think this epidemic is limited to the US, think again. DrugRehab.com states:

'More than 32 million people worldwide use opioids annually, according to the World Drug Report. Some use substances like codeine and methadone as a means of self-medication, notably for disorders such as depression...Many people who suffer with mental disorders, such as depression, ADHD and post-traumatic stress disorder, self-medicate. This often turns into a co-occurring disorder — the combination of a mental health disorder and a substance use disorder.'

In some countries, more than ten per cent of adults are prescribed antidepressants annually, according to a 2018 research paper published by the *International Journal of Mental Health Nursing*. The paper referenced a survey of 1,829 New Zealanders who had been prescribed antidepressants. Almost half (forty-four per cent) had been taking antidepressants for more than three years and were still taking them, while fifty-five per cent reported withdrawal effects when stopping medication. However, only one per cent of participants recalled being told about withdrawal effects when prescribed the drugs.

The paper (titled 'How Many of 1,829 Antidepressant Users Report Withdrawal Effects or Addiction?') states, *'Such high rates of withdrawal symptoms suggest that all concerned, including mental health nurses, need to help people considering antidepressants to understand that it can be difficult to withdraw from them. It will also be beneficial to closely monitor people already taking antidepressants and who are at risk of long-term usage.'*

According to a 2018 article published by *The New York Times*, many users who try to quit say they cannot because of withdrawal symptoms they were never warned about. These include anxiety, depression, light-headedness, tiredness and flu-like symptoms, and even electric shock sensations known as 'zaps'.

Again, this issue extends beyond the US. Across much of the developed world, long-term prescription use is on the rise. In

Britain, prescription rates have doubled over the last decade. Meanwhile, in New Zealand, a survey of long-term users found withdrawal was the most common adverse effect, cited by almost three-quarters of survey participants.

Dr Anthony Kendrick, a professor of primary care at the University of Southampton in Britain, told *The New York Times*, '*Some people are essentially being parked on these drugs for convenience's sake because it's difficult to tackle the issue of taking them off. Should we really be putting so many people on antidepressants long-term when we don't know if it's good for them, or whether they'll be able to come off?*'

The New York Times analysed data gathered since 1999 as part of a national survey on health and nutrition. The data revealed more than 34.4 million adults took antidepressants in 2013–14, up from 13.4 million in the 1999–2000 survey.

According to the *Times*, adults over forty-five, women and white people are more likely to take antidepressants than younger adults, men and minorities. The article states, '*White women over 45 account for about one-fifth of the adult population but account for 41 percent of antidepressant users, up from about 30 percent in 2000, the analysis found. Older white women account for 58 percent of those on antidepressants long term.*'

The data also established that seven per cent of American adults have taken antidepressants for at least five years. This is especially concerning when you consider that antidepressants were originally thought of as a short-term treatment, to be taken for six to nine months only.

Thankfully, alternatives are being explored. For example, cannabis – previously considered a 'deviant' drug – is now legal in eleven US states for adults over the age of twenty-one, and legal for medical use in thirty-three US states. Research suggests medicinal cannabis can reduce social anxiety and may be beneficial for improving post-traumatic stress disorder.

Even senior figures who previously opposed medicinal cannabis use are now in favour of it. This includes former House Speaker John Boehner, who, in 2018, joined the board of Acreage Holdings, which holds a portfolio of cannabis cultivation, processing and dispensing operations in the US. In April 2018, Boehner tweeted, *'I'm joining the board of #AcreageHoldings because my thinking on cannabis has evolved. I'm convinced de-scheduling the drug is needed so we can do research, help our veterans, and reverse the opioid epidemic ravaging our communities.'*

There are also grassroots community efforts such as The Withdrawal Project (TWP), run by a non-profit called the Inner Compass Initiative. The TWP website describes itself as a 'living library of wisdom', designed to help people taper off and heal from the effects of psychiatric drugs.

Addressing male midlife depression and anger

'Every man has his secret sorrows which the world knows not; and often times we call a man cold when he is only sad.'

– Henry Wadsworth Longfellow

David: One in eight men will experience depression in their lives, according to Beyond Blue, an Australian non-profit working to address mental health issues. What are the indicators? Men who are angry, irritable and agitated. Other signs and symptoms include increased risk taking, excessive crying, physical fatigue and feelings of sadness, hopelessness and inadequacy.

Research indicates that male depression peaks in midlife, possibly because of:

- Declining health and other physical changes
- Relationship breakdowns and/or family stress
- Career demands
- Financial challenges
- Personal and professional disappointments
- A lack of time for exercise, passion projects and so on
- Loneliness (we will discuss this in more detail soon)
- A growing awareness of their own mortality

Often, in a bid to mask their depression, men become angry. In an article for Main Line Health (a US-based not-for-profit health system), Dr Stephen Mechanick says, '*Culturally, men are conditioned to be more aggressive, to focus on fighting things and not to talk about feelings, which may be seen as a sign of weakness. For some men it's easier to act out anger or manifest anger in some other way.*'

In other instances, men are not even aware of the extent to which their mental health has deteriorated. In my experience, this is particularly prevalent among men who are busy, as they simply do not take any time to check in on themselves. In some cases, men avoid seeking help, as they think they are supposed to be tough, self-reliant, able to manage pain and to take charge of situations. As a result, it can be difficult for men to acknowledge they have any health problems, let alone a mental health problem.

This is particularly prevalent among men who have lost their jobs. Many of my out-of-work male colleagues have contacted me to discuss what I am doing, in terms of working for myself, and how I have gone about it. These men have had successful careers, strongly associate their personal value with their work, and, in some cases, have been searching for new employment over an extended period – without success. In a 2016 article by n-gen People Performance Inc. (which helps companies manage generational differences in the workplace), Giselle Kovary writes:

'Most Gen Xers are not old enough to completely retire immediately after [being] laid off, but they can also be considered "not young enough" to start a new role at a new organisation. Some organisations prefer to hire younger employees who, typically, command lower salaries, are seen as more "tech friendly" and are hired to "grow into" their roles.'

Feeling overlooked or replaced, many middle-aged men are suffering a crisis of confidence. However, it may not be evident to others – particularly if the man in question cannot bear to be seen as 'failing'. As a result, they may withdraw from social and professional activities out of fear of not being their usual self or doubting themselves entirely.

In a bid to address male mental health, Beyond Blue highlights the importance of community, which can help *all* men feel less lonely, more valued and, most importantly, more connected:

'Men experience loneliness more than women, and it's not just blokes living alone who get lonely. Many men feel the pressure to work hard to provide for their family, and don't get as much time to catch up with their mates as they used to....If it's hard to meet up with your mates, even texting a mate to say g'day can help make you, and them, feel more connected.

'One way to stay in touch is to join a local group – whether it's a footy team, a community group, or a weekly run or swim club, you'll find meeting new people and having a yarn will help you feel more connected to the community around you.'

For many men, creating time for this is a real challenge. I have observed men in their late thirties enter executive roles. They are in their prime, physically and professionally. But by their early forties, their physical and mental health has deteriorated. In addition to working in demanding roles, they often spend countless hours attending events after work and on the weekend, further reducing the little time they have for themselves.

When I was in my early forties, vigorous exercise was a daily priority. I either swam or ran every morning. Physically, I was the fittest I had ever been. But at the end of each year, I was utterly exhausted. Eventually, my wife said I should rethink the type of exercise I was doing. She suggested yoga.

Yoga is now my primary physical activity. I have found immense benefits, physically and mentally, but not without judgement from many of my male friends. Thankfully, more men are beginning to share their positive experiences of practising yoga. In an article for *Yoga Journal*, legendary surfer Gerry Lopez states, '*Yoga hasn't just improved my surfing; it's improved my life. Being aware, centred, and present is where we all should be. Unfortunately, most of us are not. Everybody needs yoga, but not everyone understands that.*'

For me, the unexpected benefit of practising yoga has been the community I have joined. At my local yoga studio, there is a diverse group of people, all of whom are connected through their practice. My wife refers to this group as my other family. Like me, she has her own 'other families' through some of the activities she participates in. These places of community and connection have helped us both. I would encourage others – particularly other middle-aged men – to be open to new experiences, as there may be unexpected benefits. You may even discover another 'family' that you ultimately become part of.

There are other options too. At an extended family gathering, I spoke to a retired man who explained how bored he was when he initially retired. Many of us dream of retirement – days filled doing what we want to do. However, upon leaving their place of employment, many men discover they are lonely and isolated. Eventually, this man joined his local Men's Shed, where he enjoys the interactions with other men while they work on something together.

Is there room for delayed gratification in your 'best life'?

'I do not exist to impress the world.
I exist to live my life in a way
that will make me happy.'

– Richard Bach

David: In my twenties, I met somebody who said there is a big difference between someone who *must* work in their late forties and someone who can *choose* how they work. With regard to the latter, he explained that it required the discipline of not wanting everything now, instead focusing on what you need. In my thirties, I met a successful executive who explained that he and his wife lived like students. Not in a share house, but not in an elaborate home, either. They lived well within their means. They were quietly preparing for their future. Both conversations were timely and influential.

Delayed gratification occurs when someone resists the temptation of an immediate reward in preference for a larger or more enduring reward later. In 1972, a study was conducted to understand when the control of delayed gratification develops in children. A series of children were offered a marshmallow. They were told that if they waited for a period of time and didn't eat the marshmallow, they would be offered a second marshmallow as well. In follow-up studies, the researchers found that children who were able to wait longer for the double reward tended to have better life outcomes, including higher grades and educational attainment.

Today, many people want to live their 'best life' – and they want to live it now. Social media provides a platform for people to share images or stories of their 'best life', but it may not be their real life. In many cases, it is fabricated. It is what they *want* their life to be, or what they want others to see. Unfortunately, this is just another case of 'keeping up with the Joneses'. Many people feel social pressure to drive a certain car, wear a certain style of clothes, travel to particular places and live in a specific area – and document it all for the world to see. This is not healthy or sustainable, in my opinion.

On top of that, it seems many people are perpetually in a rush – particularly when it comes to advancing their careers. That used to be me – until a mentor helped me balance the rush by explaining that your twenties are for education, your thirties are for gaining experience and your forties are for harvesting. I asked this person, 'How do you know when you can harvest?' His response was, 'You harvest when you can move between industries or move independently.'

To move independently means to be engaged by others for your expertise. This is now how I work. But it has not happened overnight. On the contrary, it has been decades in the making and required a genuine partnership with my wife, who, like me, recognised the benefits of delayed gratification. In my twenties, I spent four years at night school to complete undergraduate and postgraduate degrees. Then, in my thirties, my wife and I started our family while living in London. Raising young children in a foreign city – without family support – was challenging, but my wife and I remained committed to the bigger plan.

There have also been times in my career when work was not particularly enjoyable but offered an environment of learning. I embraced the learning, as it enabled me to acquire new knowledge and skills. Even today, within my own business, I remain very interested in the learning aspect. I regularly seek feedback from people by asking them three questions: What is going well? What needs to be better? What are you not saying? The more you do this, the less you personalise things and the greater the understanding. As you begin to discover things at a deeper level, you become less interested in fabricated things and achieve greater authenticity. For me, this is what it means to live my 'best life'.

Slowing down to ultimately speed up

'Sometimes you need to slow down to go fast.'

– Jeff Olson

David: There are times when life presents you with an opportunity to slow down and think. In 2018 – exactly thirty years after I started working – I decided to take a break. I'd had a few breaks here and there, but I'd never really stopped. My wife encouraged me to do that in 2018. And so I did. I finished work in early July, and we had a European trip booked in September. During that time, I set myself several different challenges. I completed 100 consecutive days of yoga, undertook a major declutter of our home and finally learned how to cook. Previously, with my 'busy executive schedule', I had never taken the time to cook and found lots of excuses to do other things. I know of many other men like me – they can barbecue meat or scramble eggs, but they do not cook.

However, the true benefit of stopping did not appear until our trip to Europe, on an afternoon spent by the pool in Greece. I wrote an email to one of my former colleagues, with some reflections about the time we worked together. I then started to think about what I *wanted* to do, not what I *could* do. I knew I did not want to work within specific industries or have a particular role. I also knew that if I was to do something on my own, now was the time. I had registered a domain in 2005. There was a logo in my mind, but the details of the offering were fuzzy; I had brain fog.

But by the time October rolled around, the brain fog had lifted and I launched a beta version of my business website. By January 2019, my global network had reviewed it and given me valuable feedback. Launching a website does not create value – it creates a place for people to visit if they are interested in your services. Later that year, I started to post regularly on LinkedIn, and my former colleagues began to take notice. Some of these colleagues became my first clients.

The exciting part of slowing down is that you gain clarity, which ultimately enables you to pick up speed on something that you are genuinely passionate about. And when you have passion for what you're doing, the delayed gratification is all the sweeter. At this point, I am building something that may take three, five or ten years, but I am much happier on this path than a traditional career path. I work every day, but I have the flexibility to take time away when I want to.

Embracing the Dutch concept of niksen

'I am having a good time doing nothing.'

– Phylicia Rashād

Michelle: When my husband and I lived in Melbourne, we were busy. In addition to working full-time, we went to the gym, socialised and made a point of travelling as much as we could – both within Australia and overseas. We had a high disposable income, on account of being DINKs (double income, no kids). We had savings in the bank, a growing share portfolio and relatively low debt.

And yet I never felt that we were doing enough to get ahead. I would regularly compare us to our friends, particularly in a financial sense. I would often ask myself, 'What more can we do to improve our situation?'

After we got engaged at the end of 2017, we decided it would be cool to spend a year or so living in Asia. By that stage I was working for myself, and Jase was already working remotely, so we knew we had a unique opportunity to have one last, big adventure before we got married. We also thought it would be a good way to save some money.

We set our sights on Chiang Mai – a mountainous city in northern Thailand, with a reputation as a digital nomad hotspot. (Digital nomads work online and are, therefore, location-independent.) After packing up our apartment and hugging our friends goodbye, we hopped on a plane bound for Chiang Mai on May 19, 2018. I will never forget that day – it was the same day Prince Harry married Meghan Markle.

We fell in love with Chiang Mai as soon as we arrived. It is nothing like the big, brash city of Bangkok – or the tourist playgrounds like Phuket. Framed by luscious mountain views, Chiang Mai is filled with beautiful temples, fresh food market stalls, cute coffee shops and boutique bars.

Almost instantly, the pressure we had felt to 'get ahead' dissipated and we finally allowed ourselves to slow down. Now, that is not to say we didn't do any work while we were living in Thailand. On the contrary, we both threw ourselves into a number of new work projects. But we started work later in the day, worked fewer hours and spent more time doing, well, *nothing*.

When I say 'doing nothing', I mean we would laze by the pool in our apartment complex, sit on our balcony enjoying the sunset or sip a cocktail or two together. Some mornings, I would lie on the couch in my pyjamas, simply staring out the window. Why not? I didn't need to rush off anywhere. For most of my life, I'd always had somewhere to be – school, university, work. That was no longer the case. I was now in control of my day and could carve it up however I pleased.

Allowing myself to do nothing, even if it was only for ten or fifteen minutes a day, felt liberating and grounding simultaneously. So, when I came across the Dutch concept of niksen, I felt validated – and thankful that our move to Thailand had allowed me to embrace this idea. Niksen is a Dutch proverb that literally translates as 'doing nothing'. Note that this is not the same thing as mindfulness. A *Time* article states, '*Whereas mindfulness is about being present in the moment, niksen is about carving out time to just be, even letting your mind wander rather than focusing on the details of an action.*'

According to the article, the idea of doing nothing is increasingly being framed as an effective way to combat stress and burnout. It can also help people come up with new ideas, says Ruut Veenhoven, a Dutch sociologist and a global authority on the scientific study of happiness:

> '*"Even when we 'niks,'" or do nothing, "our brain is still processing information and can use the available processing power to solve pending problems," he says, which in turn can boost one's creativity. This could manifest in having a breakthrough solution to a problem on a walk or a great business idea reveal itself while daydreaming.*'

I encourage you to try it.

Tapping into the quietness

'Quietness is the beginning of virtue.
To be silent is to be beautiful.
Stars do not make a noise.'

– James Stephens

David: The clear air at dawn helps me think; I place things in their context and then determine my actions. It is probably my favourite part of the day. I am my most productive at night, but my best thinking is at dawn. Many of my former colleagues know that I enjoy writing a weekly blog. Once upon a time, the blog was written on a Friday at dawn. There were times when I went to bed on Thursday without knowing what I was going write the following morning, but through the quietness it appeared.

For many years, my other mornings of the week were for exercise, alternating between running and swimming. When running at dawn, I do not listen to music – I focus on my breathing and being present. I loved running in the rain. The drops on my face and head felt almost therapeutic, and there were fewer people out. Now my running and swimming have been replaced by walking and yoga, which I touched on earlier. Anyone who practises yoga regularly knows that you need to become one with your thoughts. As a middle-aged professional man, I was not happy with some elements of my life and I have managed to deal with these, partly thanks to my yoga practice.

I have met men who are unhappy but do not have the time to ascertain why. Taking the time to deal with your stuff is a commitment that many do not make, either because of the confronting nature of it or the consequences. Several years ago, I was spending an extraordinary amount of time travelling for work and away from home, but this was not how I wanted to live my life with a young family.

Tapping into the quietness – by rising early to write or exercise – has enabled me to launch my business, write my first book and create a future that I am genuinely excited about. Often, my wife will accompany me on my walks; we tend to walk for about an hour. We try not to force our conversations and will often walk together in silence.

Another way I tap into the quietness is by having a shower. This may sound a little odd, but I often like to shower in the dark. After a busy day or a long flight, I find it rejuvenates me and helps me think creatively. And I am not alone, it seems. According to a study conducted by cognitive psychologist Scott Barry Kaufman, seventy-two per cent of people have experienced new ideas while in the shower. In fact, fourteen per cent of people take showers for the sole purpose of generating creative thoughts and insights. Says Kaufman, '*The calm, solitary and non-judgemental shower environment may afford creative thinking by allowing the mind to wander freely and may cause people to be more open to their inner stream of consciousness and daydreams.*'

Hygge and happiness

'*Hygge is about an atmosphere and an experience, rather than about things.*'

– **Meik Wiking**

David: There is a lot we can learn from Europe – like the concept of Janteloven, which we discussed in Chapter 3, and the idea of niksen, which Michelle touched on earlier. There is another European concept I'd like to discuss: the Danish concept of hygge. Pronounced 'hoo-ga', this term was added to the Oxford Dictionary in 2017. It refers to *'the quality of being warm and comfortable that gives a feeling of happiness'*. A 2018 *Quartz* article sums it up like this:

'[Hygge] *refers to high-quality social interactions. Hygge can be used as a noun, adjective or verb (to hygge oneself), and events and places can also be hyggelige (hygge-like).*

'Hygge is sometimes translated as "cosy," but a better definition of hygge is "intentional intimacy," which can happen when you have safe, balanced, and harmonious shared experiences. A cup of coffee with a friend in front of a fireplace might qualify, as could a summer picnic in the park.

'A family might have a hygge evening that entails board games and treats, or friends might get together for a casual dinner with dimmed lighting, good food and easy-going fun. Spaces can also be described as hyggelige ("Your new house is so hyggeligt") and a common way of telling a host thank you after a dinner is to say that it was hyggeligt (meaning, we had a good time). Most Danish social events are expected to be hyggelige, so it would be a harsh critique to say that a party or dinner wasn't hyggelige.'

It is worth pointing out that Denmark has some of the highest taxes in the world. However, it also has a stable government, low levels of public corruption, and access to high-quality education and healthcare. Meanwhile, the World Happiness Report routinely ranks Denmark as one of the happiest countries in the world.

Research has established that hygge is integral to people's sense of wellbeing. Like Janteloven, it promotes egalitarianism. Hygge is not a secret. In 2018, Amazon was selling more than 900 books on the topic, while Instagram has generated millions of posts with the hashtag #hygge. According to the *Quartz* article, hygge acts as a buffer against stress and creates a space to build camaraderie. The concept is not exclusive to the Danes, either. The Norwegians have koselig, the Swedes mysig, the Dutch gezenlligheid and the Germans gemütlichkeit.

Creating a warm environment has certainly been very important to me throughout my life, and I believe it has made me happier. For at least half of my adult life, I have lived in apartments or townhouses. My wife and I didn't move into our family home until I was almost forty; this was late for my generation. The places I have enjoyed living in were not large spaces of grandeur. On the contrary, they were often simple and, in London, un-renovated apartments that we made our home. When I reflect on my life experiences, what I *thought* I needed and what I *actually* needed are two different things. Having the *right* space – rather than having *lots* of space – has been key.

Living with less (by choice)

'The less I needed, the better I felt.'

– Charles Bukowski

Michelle: In early 2018, my husband and I decided to leave our cosy little life in the leafy suburb of Elwood, Melbourne and live overseas for a year or two. The plan was to put all our stuff in storage and only take the essentials (some of our clothes and our laptops). During the packing process, I was shocked to discover how much *stuff* we had managed to cram into our two-bedroom apartment. It was not necessarily out on display, but there were closets and drawers full of all sorts of things, often in duplicate.

I felt very relieved once every single item had been given away, thrown out or boxed up. That was almost three years ago. Jason and I have since returned to Australia, but we are currently based in Perth, where, at the time of writing, we rent a fully furnished apartment. All our worldly possessions are still sitting in a storage unit in Melbourne – and will remain there for the foreseeable future. And I can honestly say that I hardly ever think about them.

In fact, I have found living with less to be positively liberating. I feel lighter, less stressed and more relaxed. And it seems I am not alone. Minimalist living continues to rise up the ranks as a desirable lifestyle, with countless books, blog posts and articles celebrating its benefits.

A couple of years ago, I read a book titled *Everything That Remains: A Memoir by The Minimalists*. It was written by Joshua Fields Millburn and Ryan Nicodemus – who claim to have helped over twenty million people live meaningful lives with less. One of the concepts they encourage would-be minimalists to embrace is the 'Packing Party'. Ryan talks about his own experience of this in a blog post on The Minimalists website. Here is an excerpt:

> *'I didn't want to spend months slowly paring down my possessions like Josh had. That was fine for him, but I needed faster results. So we came up with a crazy idea: let's throw a Packing Party. (Everything is more fun when you put "party" at the end.) We decided to pack all my belongings as if I were moving. And then I would unpack only the items I needed over the next three weeks.*

> *'Josh came over and helped me box up everything: my clothes, my kitchenware, my towels, my electronics, my TVs, my framed photographs and paintings, my toiletries, even my furniture. Everything. We literally pretended I was moving.*

> *'After nine hours and a couple pizza deliveries, everything was packed....Each box was labelled so I'd know where to go when I needed a particular item. Labels like, "living*

room," "junk drawer #1," "kitchen utensils," "bedroom closet," "junk drawer #7." So forth and so on.

'I spent the next twenty-one days unpacking only the items I needed. My toothbrush. My bed and bedsheets. Clothes for work. The furniture I actually used. Kitchenware. A tool set. Just the things that added value to my life.

'After three weeks, 80% of my stuff was still in those boxes. Just sitting there. Unaccessed. I looked at those boxes and couldn't even remember what was in most of them. All those things that were supposed to make me happy weren't doing their job. So I donated and sold all of it.

'And you know what? I started to feel rich for the first time in my life. I felt rich once I got everything out of the way, so I could make room for everything that remains.'

Granted, the Packing Party idea may be a little too extreme for some people. But it is just one of the ways people are choosing to live with less. The other trend I have been following with interest is the tiny house movement, which advocates living simply in tiny homes, many of which are mobile.

The movement promotes financial freedom, eco-conscious living and a shift away from consumerism. It continues to gain pace all over the world, with multiple TV shows devoted to the idea. According to Tiny House Citizens, two-thirds (sixty-six per cent) of tiny home dwellers have no credit card debt, while sixty-nine per cent do not have a mortgage. Not only is a tiny home cheaper than a normal house, it forces the occupant to choose their possessions carefully. Naturally, this results in less spending, less accumulation of stuff and less debt.

What's not to like about that? I, for one, hope to be a tiny house citizen one day.

Reflection

David: This chapter is undoubtedly the heaviest, primarily as it discusses suicide. Specifically, the devastating statistics worldwide. Following on from this, we highlighted the rise and impact of prescription drugs, which are now the most abused substances in the world behind alcohol and marijuana. From there, we turned our attention to male depression, which is becoming a big problem among Gen X men in particular. Of course, there are no quick fixes for any of these issues. However, in the second half of the chapter, we explored some of the ways that might help people to reframe their perspectives – if only to help others who may be struggling. These include the Dutch concept of niksen, the Danish concept of hygge and the idea of living with less.

When reflecting on this chapter, consider:

- Have you been affected, either directly or indirectly, by suicide and/or prescription drug use? How did this impact you?
- What are your thoughts on the extent of male midlife depression and anger in our community?
- How could you support a male in your life who appears to be undergoing a crisis of confidence?
- Do you feel pressure to maintain a certain image within your community? Is this pressure exacerbated by social media?
- When was the last time you stopped – *truly* stopped – in order to reassess and, if necessary, change the direction of your life?
- Would you consider trying the concept of niksen? Why or why not?
- What about hygge? Why or why not?
- What are your thoughts on the minimalist movement and tiny homes? Could you see yourself doing either of these things? Why or why not?
- When it comes to your home, what do you need? What could you go without?

CHAPTER 6

Living in the Land Down Under

*'Mates such as they must
stand by one another.'*

– Mary Grant Bruce

Michelle: In this chapter, David and I start by exploring notions of masculinity and femininity within Australia, and their impact not only on individuals but on entire communities. We also discuss loneliness, which is an increasingly modern-day battle and certainly not one Australians are immune to. David also highlights the benefits of volunteering, which, sadly, is in decline across the country.

Our masculine society and what it means

*'I think of masculine and feminine energy like
two sides to a battery. There's a plus side and
a minus side, and in order to make something
turn on, you need to have opposites touching.'*

– Tracy McMillan

Michelle: One of the things that can really cripple Australian communities, I think, is the fact that Australian society as a whole is quite masculine. Now, before you dismiss that as a throwaway comment without any backup, hear me out. There is actual research that indicates some societies are more masculine or feminine.

The research comes from Finnish company Hofstede Insights, which has scored countries across six cultural dimensions (this is known as the 6-D Model). The score range runs from zero to 100, with 50 as a mid-level.

Here is a brief outline of the six dimensions:

1. **Power distance:** The extent to which the less powerful members of institutions and organisations within a country expect and accept that power is distributed unequally.
2. **Individualism:** The degree of interdependence a society maintains among its members.
3. **Masculinity:** The extent to which society is driven by competition, achievement and success, with success defined as being the 'winner' or 'best in the field'. This is in contrast to a feminine society, where the dominant values are caring for others and quality of life.
4. **Uncertainty avoidance:** The extent to which the members of a culture feel threatened by ambiguous or unknown situations and have created beliefs and institutions that try to avoid these.
5. **Long-term orientation:** The extent to which a society has to maintain some links with its own past while dealing with the challenges of the present and future.
6. **Indulgence:** The extent to which people try to control their desires and impulses.

Here's how Australia scored across all six dimensions:

An insight into Australian culture through the lens of the 6-D Model

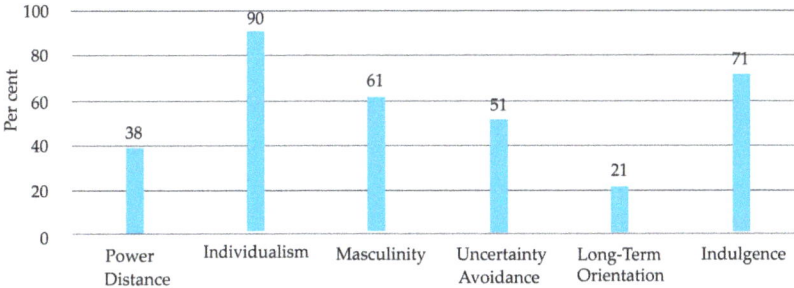

Source: Hofstede Insights

As you can see, Australia scored highly in individualism, indulgence and masculinity. On the topic of individualism, Hofstede said Australia has as a 'highly individualist culture', which *'translates into a loosely-knit society in which the expectation is that people look after themselves and their immediate families.'* On the topic of indulgence, Hofstede said Australia is an indulgent country in the sense that people *'generally exhibit a willingness to realise their impulses and desires with regard to enjoying life and having fun'* and *'act as they please and spend money as they wish.'*

These insights are interesting, but the commentary on masculinity is, in my opinion, the most insightful:

'Australia...is considered a "Masculine" society. Behaviour in school, work, and play are based on the shared values that people should "strive to be the best they can be" and that "the winner takes all". Australians are proud of their successes and achievements in life...Conflicts are resolved at the individual level and the goal is to win.'

This innate desire to win and 'be the best' is seen to varying degrees in a number of Australian industries, but none more so than sport. In *Australian Sport – Better by Design? The Evolution of Australian Sport Policy*, the authors write:

> 'For a small country...and geographically isolated from the rest of the world, sporting success is a highly visible and potent way of achieving global media exposure and international awareness.

> '...Australians also like their sporting heroes to be extra-ordinary in the sense that they should both win against the world's best, and symbolise sport's working-class traditions and tribal relations. Australian sporting larrikins are revered for their indifference to authority, loud humour, and "heavy drinking". There is, however, a downside to this hyper-masculine and sporting ethos. In addition to its tendency to marginalise the participation of women, it can produce chronic displays of poor sportsmanship and crass behaviour.'

Now, I am not suggesting Australia should end its love affair with sport (as if that would ever happen!). But on the topic of masculinity, I do think we can strive for a more balanced society. And the way we do this is by learning from other, more 'feminine' societies. According to Hofstede, the country with the least masculine society is Sweden, which received a score of just five for the masculinity dimension. That is one *twelfth* of the score Australia received! So, what does a feminine society look like? There are elements that can be applied not only on a community level but in the workplace too. Hofstede also refers to Jante Law (which we discussed in Chapter 3):

> 'A Feminine society is one where quality of life is the sign of success and standing out from the crowd is not admirable... In Feminine countries it is important to keep the life/work balance and you make sure that all are included.

'...The whole culture is based around "lagom", which means something like not too much, not too little, not too noticeable, everything in moderation. Lagom ensures that everybody has enough and nobody goes without. Lagom is enforced in society by "Jante Law" which should keep people "in place" at all times. It is a fictional law and a Scandinavian concept which counsels people not to boast or try to lift themselves above others.'

Fighting male stereotypes and toxic masculinity

'There's so much toxic masculinity out there. I grew up with the notion that the more masculine you are and the less you show emotion, the more of a man you are.'

– Karamo Brown

David: Australian men are often associated with a particular stereotype. That is, a man who's tall and fit-looking, blond, blue-eyed and Caucasian. I have experienced firsthand what it feels like to be stereotyped in this way. In the early 2000s, while my wife and I lived in London, I remember participating in a multiday coaching certification workshop for the company I was employed at.

All participants were encouraged to provide one another with feedback. One piece of feedback from a very senior colleague, which surprised me, was along the lines of, 'You should be more like Steve Irwin.' I laughed when I heard this, but I instantly felt frustrated and misunderstood – especially as the feedback came from reasonably senior people within the company. My wife and I had been living in the UK for a couple of years by this point – yet I was unable to break away from the Australian male stereotype. I was pigeonholed!

Also, was this what people were expecting from me? And what would happen if I did not meet their expectations? Would I be expected to 'revert' to fit the stereotype of the Aussie larrikin – a stereotype that is not always looked on favourably? For example, just one day after the death of Steve Irwin, Australian writer and feminist Germaine Greer wrote a scathing review of Irwin's behaviour in an article for *The Guardian* titled 'That sort of self-delusion is what it takes to be a real Aussie larrikin'.

Of course, Germaine Greer is not the first woman to attack a man (Aussie larrikin or not) so openly. In May 2020, an article by *The Lily*, which is published by *The Washington Post*, told the story of a woman who gave up her job as a tech CEO to be a full-time mother, as she was not sure her stay-at-home husband could handle it. In response to the article, Australian feminist writer Clementine Ford tweeted, '*Honestly, the coronavirus isn't killing men fast enough*'.

What do men do in these instances? In my experience, not much. Why? Often, they are concerned about saying the wrong thing or being accused of being out of step. For many men, they simply do not want to show they're hurt by such remarks. As a Generation X male, I – along with many of my peers – avoid speaking out. Instead, we may discuss certain topics in private and then say, 'Well, I'm not opening *that* can of worms.' Many men choose to sit out of certain conversations, as they feel it is easier to stay silent.

Other men may fall victim to what is known as 'toxic masculinity', which refers to traditional ideals surrounding manhood, including toughness, aggression, a suppression of emotion, dominance and stoicism. A 2018 report by the American Psychological Association states, '*Traditional masculinity ideology has been shown to limit males' psychological development, constrain their behaviour, result in gender role strain and gender role conflict and negatively influence mental health and physical health.'*

This makes me wonder: What example are my friends and I setting for our sons – and what impact will this have on them?

According to the Man Box – a study that focuses on the attitudes to manhood and the behaviours of young Australian men (aged eighteen to thirty) – sixty-nine per cent of young men agree that society expects men to act strong. Almost two-thirds (sixty per cent) agree men are expected to fight back when pushed, while more than half (fifty-six per cent) agree there is an expectation for men to never refuse sex.

In a 2014 article published by Southern Cross University, Dr Paul Edwards – who has explored male adolescent experiences and expressions of anger – said his research indicates that within Australia, a high value is placed on the idea of 'being a man', with men often told to 'man up' and or not be 'soft'. These are all terms I have heard a lot during my life.

Dr Edwards said, *'Aggression has been an endorsed expression of anger within Australian culture for young men. The purpose of anger management programs is to help young men see that they are responsible for their actions....But when anger is reinforced culturally and by the metaphors used to talk about anger, these young guys have got no reason to think this will ever change.'*

For our son, it is important that he sees beyond the Aussie male stereotype. It is also important that he sees himself outside the 'Man Box'. The Man Box is not just a study, as referenced earlier. It is also *'a set of beliefs within and across society that place pressure on men to be a certain way – to be tough; not to show any emotions; to be the breadwinner, to always be in control, use violence to solve problems; and to have many sexual partners.'*

The study reveals that men who most strongly agree with these 'rules' report poorer levels of mental health, engage in risky drinking, are more likely to be in car accidents and are more likely to commit acts of violence, online bullying and sexual harassment. The pressure to 'be a man' is everywhere in Australian society and is often reinforced by young men's closest relationships with their families, friends and partners.

There is a need to change how masculinity is viewed in Australia. Awareness of the 'Man Box' – and the damage it does – is a start. The harm extends beyond men; it contributes to ongoing sexism and male privilege in our society. We need more conversations with men and boys on this topic, so they can develop and embrace their own ideas of what it is to be a man, rather than feeling boxed in by a stereotype. In the US, an initiative called Manhood 2.0 is designed to engage young men in questioning and challenging harmful norms, and ultimately aims to transform them. Perhaps there is an opportunity to introduce something similar in Australia.

Australian alcohol use and the harm done to others

'We have a drinking game in Australia – it's called drinking.'

– Jim Jefferies

David: My wife is an emergency nurse, and, sadly, she has to manage the outcomes of excessive drinking. She now chooses not to work on weekend evenings or days of big events. She doesn't understand why some male friends insist that another male remains in a drinking round when he doesn't want or need another drink. If she is out with her girlfriends and misses a round, they are supportive. Maybe I need a couple of different friends! But research indicates this is common.

For many men and women, a night out with friends often involves drinking. In a 2019 poll conducted by FARE (the Foundation for Alcohol Research and Education), forty-seven per cent of Australians admitted they drink to get drunk. Overall, however, the attitude towards drinking is improving, with sixty-three per cent of Australians limiting their drinking to two standard drinks. Young adults and university students are also drinking less than the same age group in 2007.

According to an Insider Guides article on Australia's drinking culture, it can be difficult to refuse a drink from family and friends. The article even offers suggestions on ways to turn down drinks 'without offending anyone', which highlights the extent to which drinking is normalised in Australian culture.

Statistics show alcohol consumption is higher in Australian sporting clubs than in the broader community. Research from University of Queensland (UQ) Business School found that alcohol is widespread within sporting clubs and is often accessible to underage players in senior teams, especially as part of the socialising aspect after a game.

Millions of Australians are involved in community sport, and the clubs they are involved in often depend on alcohol sales and sponsorship. Sport is a very big part of Australian life, as it allows people of all ages the opportunity to improve their fitness, build confidence and meet new people. But when it comes to alcohol consumption within this environment, there is a lack of regulation. For example, a study by one UQ Business School doctoral student found five of the sixteen sporting clubs she interviewed did not have an alcohol policy specific to their club.

Sports marketing expert Dr Sarah Kelly said, '*Regulators, sports associations and policy makers need to work together to find ways to help clubs reduce the cultural and financial reliance upon alcohol, and promote health. Managing this critical health and social issue is all the more complex given that many teams are a mix of underage and adult players. We need a more unified and sustainable effort if we are ever to solve the problem of alcohol in sport.*'

Alcohol is not just a problem in the context of Australian sport.

According to the FARE poll, most Australians are concerned about alcohol, with sixty-six per cent indicating they believe Australia has a problem with excess drinking or alcohol abuse. More than half (fifty-three per cent) believe alcohol-related problems in Australia will worsen or remain the same over the next five to ten years, while seventy-five per cent believe more needs to be done to reduce the harm caused by alcohol. This last sentiment has remained relatively consistent over the past ten years, the study shows.

Frighteningly, more than a third of Australians (thirty-eight per cent) indicate they have been affected by alcohol-related violence, including eighteen per cent who have been victims of alcohol-related violence. Almost a quarter (twenty-three per cent) of parents or guardians with a child under eighteen report that their child has been harmed or put at risk of harm because of someone else's drinking.

In 2019, the World Health Organisation, along with several other organisations, issued a report titled 'Harm to Others from Drinking: Patterns in Nine Societies'. In general, men and younger people are strongly represented among those who did alcohol-related harm to others. A higher severity of harm was caused to people in the same household. More than a quarter of the harmful drinkers were estimated to drink more than seven standard drinks a day, and the most harmful drinkers were generally more frequent drinkers than the general population. Looking at Australia specifically, the report found that although alcohol consumption is declining, *harm* from alcohol consumption is increasing.

According to the report, this includes '*an array of negative experiences, including generalised issues such as fear and disruption due to strangers' drinking, and more specific, concrete harms such as violence, neglect or damage to property (Laslett et al. 2010). The cost of harm experienced by someone other than the drinker has been estimated at over AU$6 billion per year (Laslett et al. 2010).*'

The Alcohol and Drug Foundation (ADF) found that young people who are exposed to parental alcohol consumption are at a higher risk of initiating alcohol use. It says parents and other carers can role model lower-risk drinking practices by having regular meals together as a family to increase communication and cohesion, knowing their young person's whereabouts and who their friends are, having open conversations about alcohol use and providing clear guidelines or expectations, and modelling behaviour that they expect from their young person.

Power, uncertainty and long-term orientation

'People don't want to embrace culture shifts because it's not going to happen in the next 20 minutes.'

– Gary Vaynerchuk

Michelle: Earlier, I focused on the areas where Australia scored highly in the Hofstede 6-D model, with a particular focus on masculinity. But what about the other areas – 'power distance', 'uncertainty avoidance' and 'long-term orientation'? What do lower scores in these areas say about Australian culture and communities?

Let's discuss each one now, starting with power distance. This relates to the fact that '*all individuals in societies are not equal*', and whether that inequality is '*endorsed by the followers as much as by the leaders.*' Fortunately, Australia received a low score of 36 for this dimension. While hierarchies do exist – like in organisations, for example – they are established for convenience, says Hofstede.

On the topic of uncertainty avoidance, the verdict was less clear. To recap, this is '*the extent to which the members of a culture feel threatened by ambiguous or unknown situations and have created beliefs and institutions that try to avoid these.*' According to Hofstede, uncertainty avoidance relates to the way that a society deals with the fact that the future can never be known. This can lead to anxiety, which different cultures have learned to deal with in different ways. Australia scored 51 on this dimension, so it is sitting right in the middle. Is there a way we can move towards a lower score, though? Sweden, for example, scored 29, making it a 'low UAI society'. According to Hofstede:

> '*Low UAI societies maintain a more relaxed attitude in which practice counts more than principles and deviance from the norm is more easily tolerated. In societies exhibiting low UAI, people believe there should be no more rules than are necessary and if they are ambiguous or do not work they should be abandoned or changed. Schedules are flexible, hard work is undertaken when necessary but not for its own sake, precision and punctuality do not come naturally, innovation is not seen as threatening.*'

Finally, on the topic of long-term orientation, Australia scored just 21 and, therefore, has a normative society. Hofstede states, '*People in such societies have a strong concern with establishing the absolute Truth; they are normative in their thinking. They exhibit great respect for traditions, a relatively small propensity to save for the future, and a focus on achieving quick results.'*

In my view, this is consistent with Australia's tendency towards short-termism, which is often discussed in the context of the economy and productivity (as we touched on in Chapter 2), but less so in the context of society. Compare Australia to a country like the Netherlands, which received a considerably higher score of 67 in this dimension. According to Hofstede, this indicates the Netherlands has a pragmatic nature, whereby people *'show an ability to easily adapt traditions to changed conditions, a strong propensity to save and invest, thriftiness and perseverance in achieving results.'*

Perhaps one of the reasons why Australia has a normative society is because Australians care too much what others think – about their careers, their relationships, their parenting and so on. David explores this idea further in the next section.

Caring less what others think

> *'I care not what others think of what I do, but I care very much about what I think of what I do! That is character!'*
>
> **– Theodore Roosevelt**

David: When you are working within an organisation, there is an expectation of fitting in. Some people are better suited to certain organisations – and certain sectors – than others. For example, although I have spent over half of my career working within the financial services sector, I feel much more suited to technology and engineering type organisations. I am not an engineer. However, most of my clients are within the construction and engineering industries.

I am also someone who likes to solicit feedback from others. Many people shy away from feedback, partly because they give too much weight to it. Somebody once advised me that you can choose to do what you want with the feedback; you don't need to action anything if it doesn't feel right. In other words, try not to care too much what other people think. Avoid letting other people's thoughts and opinions cloud your own.

Gary Vaynerchuk, also known as Gary Vee, is a serial entrepreneur and bestselling author. He wrote an article for his website titled 'How to stop caring what others think'. Here is a snippet:

> '*To have a winner's mentality, you have to stop caring what other people think. You've gotta get quiet in your own head… At the core of it, the barriers so many people have aren't really about "money" or "time." They're about opinions. It's the biggest reason so many people are unhappy right now. Because they value someone else's opinion more than their own. Once you get past that, life can get real good.*'

One of the ways to do that, says Gary, is to add context to other people's feedback:

> '*The best way to take feedback is to understand where the feedback is coming from. What's the agenda behind the feedback? What's the intent? For example, so many parents tell their kids what direction they should go in their lives. But parents have an agenda too. Many parents are insecure, and use their kids' success to justify their own self-esteem.*
>
> '…*The truth is, no one has 100% context on your life outside of you. The reason I don't value my wife's or my mom's opinion more than my own is because they don't know 100%*

of everything. I have empathy for their opinions because I understand how they could come to their conclusions with limited context. But I don't take those opinions to heart.'

I encourage you to add context to the feedback of others – regardless of where the feedback is coming from (family members, friends, work colleagues and so on). It is natural to care about the opinions of people you're close to. However, sometimes, these opinions can dictate your actions and have a negative impact on your life.

Personally, sometime in the last five years, I decided it was important for me to do what I *wanted* to do, rather than meeting the expectations of others. So, after thirty years in the corporate world, I went out on my own. I feel so free as a result. This freedom is not without moments of doubt. When these moments occur, I step back from what I am doing and choose to do something that I know will make me feel better. Also, I choose to spend time with people who are optimistic, who are building as I am or who have a genuine interest in me being my best self – not what they would like me to be.

Loneliness: An increasingly modern-day battle

> *'Loneliness is the poverty of self;*
> *solitude is the richness of self.'*
>
> **– May Sarton**

Michelle: I have never lived alone, but many of my family members do – including my mother and my mother-in-law. They all cite loneliness as their biggest struggle. But you do not have to live alone to experience loneliness. According to the Australian Loneliness

Report, which highlights the loneliness levels of Australians, and the impact on their health and wellbeing, loneliness is different to feeling alone:

> 'We can be surrounded by others but still lonely, or we can be alone but not feel lonely. Loneliness may be a sign that a person's relationships are inadequate or don't meet their expectations or needs.

> 'As humans are essentially social animals, loneliness is thought to arise because an innate need to belong to a group is unmet. Loneliness signals a need to form a meaningful connection with others. Research has found that loneliness is related more to the quality than the quantity of relationships. A lonely person feels that their relationships are not meaningful and that he or she is not understood by others.'

The report reveals that one in four Australian adults are lonely. Half of those surveyed sometimes or always feel alone, while more than half (fifty-five per cent) feel they lack companionship at least sometimes. It may come as a surprise to learn that this number is highest in young adults (sixty-two per cent) compared to seniors (forty-six per cent).

According to Elisabeth Shaw, CEO of Relationships Australia NSW, an increasingly broad range of people feel lonely – for an increasingly broad range of reasons. 'We've got to get out of that stereotype that it's only elderly people that are lonely,' Ms Shaw told ABC Everyday in 2018. 'It's the under-65 people who've lost their partner. It's the single parent. It's the youth.'

Job loss or a major life change can also cause loneliness. According to Relationships Australia, being employed is consistently associated with lower rates of loneliness for both men and women. On the flip side, men who are unemployed or on income support benefits are very lonely, as are women aged twenty-five to twenty-nine. In Australia, this coincides with the average age of becoming a first-time mum.

Sadly, the Australian Loneliness Report reveals nearly thirty per cent of Australians rarely or never feel part of a group of friends, while one in four do not feel they have a lot in common with the people around them. One in five rarely or never feel close to people, while one in five say they cannot find companionship when they want it.

According to the report, Australians with higher levels of loneliness have significantly worse physical and mental health than those with lower levels of loneliness. For example, they are more likely to experience depression and to feel anxious about social interactions. It works the other way too. Those experiencing depression and/or social interaction anxiety are more likely to feel lonely.

How does being lonely increase the risk of mental health problems?

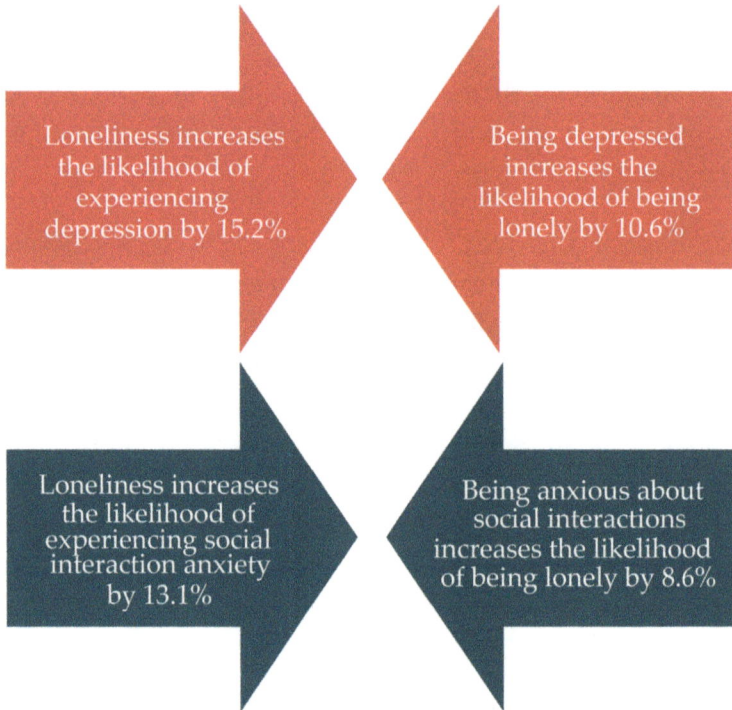

Loneliness increases the likelihood of experiencing depression by 15.2%

Being depressed increases the likelihood of being lonely by 10.6%

Loneliness increases the likelihood of experiencing social interaction anxiety by 13.1%

Being anxious about social interactions increases the likelihood of being lonely by 8.6%

Source: Australian Loneliness Report

While most Australians (ninety-two per cent) have at least one friend that they see at least once a month, it seems the days of seeking neighbourly advice are almost over. Three-quarters of Australians never or seldom have a neighbour to talk to, while eighty-two per cent say their neighbours rarely or never consult with them.

The statistics may seem grim, but that does not mean loneliness can't be overcome. The Australian Psychological Society has the following tips to help you connect with others in meaningful ways:

- **Think positive.** Don't worry about how you are perceived. Instead, shift your focus to the other person or the topic of conversation.
- **Don't compare.** When it comes to social interactions, remember that quality and enjoyment matter more than quantity.
- **Expect change.** Relationships shift over time. Accepting change as normal can help you adjust.
- **Tolerate discomfort.** Socialising can feel awkward sometimes, but it doesn't mean you're doing anything wrong. The more you reach out to others, the more your skills will improve.
- **Practise listening.** Make a point of asking people questions and really listening to their answers, rather than just waiting for a turn to talk.
- **Rehearse questions.** Spend some time thinking about questions you can ask if and when conversation stalls. For example, questions related to hobbies, travel, career and so on.
- **Use names.** It may seem obvious, but using someone's name – once you know it – shows you care. Offer your name as well.
- **Get offline.** Social media definitely has a role to play in helping people connect, but it's important to establish offline connections too.
- **Start chatting.** Pluck up the courage to chat to strangers – perhaps a fellow commuter or dog walker – and see if you can find any common ground.
- **Help someone.** Create a bond with someone by offering help or asking for it.

- **Join in.** Embrace opportunities to join a group, volunteer for a cause or participate in an activity. This provides an easy way to get to know people, as there's a shared focus.
- **Reach out.** Consider catching up with friends or colleagues from your past – perhaps in a place where you shared happy memories.
- **Manage stress.** If you suffer from social interaction anxiety, use simple stress management techniques to help calm your nerves, like breathing deeply.
- **Keep practising.** Remember that social connections are good for you, but they also take time to develop. Keep practising and don't be discouraged.

Learning to embrace and manage loneliness

'Loneliness adds beauty to life. It puts a special burn on sunsets and makes night air smell better.'

– Henry Rollins

David: Loneliness is a problem for many people; I have been lonely in my life. I have felt lonely when I have had many people around me, and when I have been a part of a community. Some of those communities were just wrong for me. Sometimes I knew they were wrong, and other times I had to learn they were wrong. Those communities were not bad; they worked well for others, just not me. In my thirties, I discovered that a diverse community feeds my soul. When I lived in London, I was part of an exercise community at a local council gym and remain friends with many of these people. Today, I am part of a local yoga community in Melbourne, and I'm also part of an international technology community – an eclectic mix of people that I have met throughout my career.

In 1977, my mother passed away when I was six. Losing a parent results in loneliness. I have felt a hollow for much of my life as a result. Many have helped fill the hollow, and they have done a fabulous job, but there is something still empty. The void in my life will probably always be there. I look at my children now and think about what my mum has missed, and what my children have missed too.

My father remarried in 1979; I have stepsiblings, and we all get on well. There have been subsequent events that have challenged our stepfamily, and the beautiful thing is that we have all come together to work through it. This is probably due to not living in each other's pockets – we are busy with our own families, and all have very different interests.

My loneliness resulted in fantasy play when I was a child. I would close my eyes, pretending I was somewhere else, doing something else. Without a doubt, it affected my attention span. I would be called a daydreamer. However, when I escaped into my head, I thought about things a lot. I believe this escapism has helped me deal better with things in the real world. Professionally, I deal with complex problems. My brain operates in halves – one half in the room and the other half off processing. I think it is a learned skill; it was refined when I attended eight schools over ten years.

I also like to travel by myself, and I have been fortunate to take many solo international work trips. Some of my former colleagues used to worry whether I would be okay on my own. My response? Definitely. Also, I was quietly upset when they made Wi-Fi available on planes, as it means I am contactable. This eats into my thinking time.

As Michelle just touched on, loneliness is a problem in our modern life – there are many people who live in big cities, with people all around them, and yet they are lonely. I can relate to that. One way to alleviate this is to focus on 'weak ties'. That is, casual acquaintances at your local coffee shop, gym, office and so on. These interactions, although small, can make a big difference to your life.

A 2020 BBC article highlights the benefits of weak ties, referencing a 1973 paper by sociology professor Mark Granovetter, titled 'The Strength of Weak Ties'. The article states:

> *'One way to think about any person's social world is that you have an inner circle of people whom you often talk to and feel close with, and an outer circle of acquaintances whom you see infrequently or fleetingly. Granovetter named these categories "strong ties" and "weak ties". His central insight was that for new information and ideas, weak ties are more important to us than strong ones.'*

Weak-tie encounters can boost mental wellbeing too. The article cited the research of Gillian Sandstrom, a senior lecturer in psychology at the University of Essex, who investigated the extent to which people derive happiness from weak-tie relationships:

> *'She asked a group of respondents to keep a record of all their social interactions over the course of several different days. She found that participants with larger networks of weak ties tended to be happier overall, and that on days when a participant had a greater number of casual interactions with weak ties – a local barista, a neighbour, a member of yoga class – they experienced more happiness and a greater sense of belonging.'*

Volunteering feeds the soul, but it's in decline

'Research has shown that people who volunteer often live longer.'

– Allen Klein

David: I have volunteered on occasions throughout my life, but not nearly enough. At times when I did volunteer in the past, I felt compelled to do it but was not committed. The compelling feeling was due to an expectation that this is the right thing to do. However, the commitment was missing due to a lack of connection.

For the past six years, I have volunteered at my university. I am exceptionally grateful to Swinburne University, which accepted me as a mature-age student and provided a pathway for my under- and postgraduate study. Without these qualifications, I would not have been able to pursue such a rewarding career, which has enabled the work I do now.

Beyond several annual meetings and the lecturing I undertake, I immensely enjoy the events I attend. I have an emotional connection to the campus. Beyond the opportunities I have been provided, the university is located only several blocks away from where my mother lived, attended primary school and danced with my father at the local town hall. This connection provides a warm feeling in my belly.

Many organisations are dependent on volunteering from large charities, political parties and sporting clubs. Volunteers contribute billions to the economy and are one of the forces keeping our society alive. The benefits of volunteering are two-way – research has found that volunteers enjoy greater levels of mental and physical wellbeing.

However, in 2015, Volunteering Australia shared data from the Australian Bureau of Statistics (ABS), which revealed volunteering rates were declining for the first time in almost twenty years, with seventy-five per cent of people surveyed saying they feel rushed or pressed for time. According to the ABS, thirty-one per cent of Australians volunteered in 2014, compared to thirty-six per cent in 2010. Separate research from the Productivity Commission shows Australia suffered a ten per cent decline in the number of volunteer firefighters between 2009 and 2019. In the same time frame, the total proportion of volunteers, including firefighters and support staff, dropped from 1,015 per 100,000 people to 824. That is a reduction of almost twenty per cent.

In a 2019 ABC Everyday article, Australian social researcher Rebecca Huntley said she doubts Australians care less about their community than they used to, stating the decline is *more likely to be the result of pressure on people's schedules and bank balances.* According to the article, volunteering is high among those aged fifteen to seventeen (forty-two per cent) and those aged sixty-five to seventy-five (thirty-five per cent). Those aged thirty-five to forty-four are also likely to volunteer, perhaps via kids' activities and interests. Says Huntley:

> *Certainly older and younger people are the ones with more time than the harried middle-aged cohort...Many of us are doing unpaid caring work for family members, younger and older. And some of us are taking on a second job to keep the family afloat.*

> *It's not always about available time, though. People employed part-time have a higher volunteer rate than people not in the labour force. All of this points to the fact that you*

need to have the combination of time and money to be able to volunteer.'

Several of my previous employers made volunteering days available to their employees, but I have only seen one realise the benefits. Volunteering was part of the organisation's culture; the founder had established a charity based on something they felt strongly about. This emotional connection resulted in storytelling and inspired others to become involved.

Reflection

David: In this chapter, we launched straight into the idea of masculine versus feminine societies, with research showing Australia is very much the former. From there, we moved into a discussion on male stereotypes and toxic masculinity. We also highlighted the extent of alcohol use (or abuse) among Australians, and some of the impacts of this. In the second half of the chapter, we discussed a range of factors shaping Australian communities, including loneliness and the sad decline of volunteering.

When reflecting on this chapter, consider:

- Do you think Australia is a masculine society? Why or why not?
- What are your thoughts on male stereotypes and toxic masculinity within Australia? How might we address these issucs?
- To what extent are you affected by alcohol use, either your own and/or others'?
- What are you doing in your life to meet the expectations of others?
- How could you start to make small changes to move closer to what you *want* to do, rather than what might be expected of you?

- Are you, or is someone you know, affected by loneliness? In what way/s?
- Who in your life volunteers? What causes do they volunteer for, and why?
- Where would you like to volunteer? Which causes would benefit most from having you as a volunteer, and why?

PART 4

FAMILY

CHAPTER 7

Every Boy and Girl in the World

*'If you want to change the world,
go home and love your family.'*

– Mother Teresa

Michelle: In this chapter, David and I offer different perspectives on family as we highlight some of the challenges facing our respective generations. For Gen X, these include the myth of 'perfecting parenting' (perpetuated by social media), navigating their role as the sandwich generation, and determining how best to prepare their children for an increasingly complex future. For Gen Y, pressures include the many dilemmas of parenthood (including whether or not to have children, and why) and – like Gen X – the responsibilities that come with being 'sandwiched' by young children on one side and ageing parents on the other.

Will Gen Z face the same struggles as Gen Y?

*'I think the kids that struggle are
way more prepared for real life.'*

– Jimmy John Liautaud

David: People are living longer than they used to and, in many cases, are still living full, active lives past the age of sixty-five. As a result, major life events – like having children – are increasingly being delayed. In my stepfamily, my father and stepmother are almost the same age. My stepmother had her first child at twenty-one, whereas my father was in his thirties when he became a father. I was like my father; my first child also arrived when I was in my mid-thirties. Meanwhile, my elder stepsiblings had their children young, like my stepmother. At our extended family gatherings, my parents have great-grandchildren and grandchildren the same age.

All parents just want their children to be happy. However, parents also set expectations for their children, either consciously or unconsciously. I have been guilty of both; my wife less so. How? My wife and I decided that our three children should all attend different high schools. They are all different and what might be suitable for one child is not ideal for another. It may have been easier to send all our children to the same school, but we believe this may compromise their ability to realise their potential.

It is unlikely I will meet my great-grandchildren, as my parents have, as my wife and I had our children late. Like anything, there are pros and cons. On the plus side, we lived abroad and have travelled a little more than our siblings. Maybe our life experience has influenced some of our choices as a result. I am not saying we are more enlightened, but our thinking is a little different. We hope these choices may help our children realise their life's purpose earlier than I did, although this is a work in progress.

As a father of three school-aged children (members of Generation Z), I often ask myself: What comes after their education? How prepared will our children be to deal with the world they will live in? I am aware of some of the struggles faced by the generation preceding theirs – the Millennial, or Gen Y, generation.

In a 2018 article for *The Guardian*, Gen Y freelancer Juliana Piskorz spoke candidly about her 'quarter-life crisis'. Juliana kicked off the article with a reference to her fifteen-year-old self's diary, in which she outlined a series of goals she wished to achieve by the age of twenty-five. These included owning a house in Notting Hill (an affluent district of West London), being a successful TV presenter, being engaged and owning an Audi. She then goes on to say:

> *'I am 25 and a half; single, unable to pay my rent and the closest thing I own to a car is a broken skateboard.*

> *'...I'm in the throes of a quarter-life crisis. A very different animal to its middle-aged cousin, mostly because no one aged 26 can afford a vintage Jag and is unlikely to have progressed far enough in their career to have a secretary to shag. The quarter-life crisis, or my experience of it, manifests itself in me wanting to run away; to start again; or bury myself in anything that will distract me from my own reality. Clinical psychologist Alex Fowke defines it as "a period of insecurity, doubt and disappointment surrounding your career, relationships and financial situation" in your 20s. Check, check, check.'*

Worryingly, Juliana is not alone. A 2017 LinkedIn study revealed seventy-two per cent of young Brits have experienced a quarter-life crisis, while 32.4 per cent said they were currently having one. Today, the stages of life have changed. As Juliana points out, her grandmother was married with children at twenty-one (like my stepmother), whereas a twenty-one-year-old today is likely to still live at home with their parents.

In the 1980s, once you left university, you could afford to service a small mortgage. This was an event that indicated you were well on your way to the stages of fully fledged adulthood. Currently, this is not possible for many millennials. Their visions for their lives are different to those of the past, which had clear markers of adulthood in the form of home ownership, marriage and children. These are now being delayed – or put off entirely – due to unaffordable housing, reduced job security and lower incomes.

In her article, Juliana includes a quote from Dr James Arkell, a consultant psychiatrist at the Nightingale Hospital in London, who said he is often surprised at his young patients' lack of self-esteem:

> *'Very often 20-somethings I see here are beautiful, talented and have the world on a plate, but they don't like themselves and that's got to be about society making them feel as if they have to keep up with these unrelenting standards.'*

Juliana has tried to have this conversation with her parents, who do not understand why she spends so much time worrying about where she is in life. Their advice is: 'If you can't afford your rent get a new job' or 'Move out of London'. Juliana's conclusion is that her parents' relationships with their jobs are motivated by financial security rather than ideological fulfilment. As a parent, this concerns me. My wife and I want to encourage our children to explore their passions – albeit balanced with some realities of life.

How we explain these realities is a challenge. One of the reasons for this is the inescapable prevalence of social media in young people's lives, which has created a culture of comparison that often leads to anxiety and, in some cases, full-blown panic. Juliana touches on this in her article:

> *'The smallest things set me off: an Instagram post announcing a friend's engagement; finding out a celebrity I fancy is several years younger than me; Monday mornings; anyone "living their best life" on a beach. The idea that people are "achieving" while I flounder fills me with panic.'*

So, is it too late to turn things around? Perhaps not. According to Dr Arkell, it ultimately comes down to acceptance. He states, '*You can go faster and faster and faster and get nowhere. Sometimes it's important to accept your life for how it is now, even if it's not where you want to be yet.*' This is something my wife and I will try to instil in our children, particularly as they enter adulthood.

Social media and the myth of the perfect parent

'Perfectionism is a self-destructive and addictive belief system.'

– Brené Brown

David: When my wife and I moved to London in 2001, we communicated with our family and friends via email. We would send semi-regular updates, accompanied by a few pictures. When we left London in 2010, there was a range of social media and content sharing platforms. Despite now living on the other side of the world, we remain very connected, by sharing and liking posts.

But there is a dark side of social media. Specifically, the pressure to present a picture-perfect life, when the reality may be different. According to the RealLife parenting study, carried out by Scottish organisation Home-Start, six out of ten parents feel pressure from social media to be the 'perfect parent', while half would put off seeking help out of fear of being seen as a bad parent.

In a 2019 article for *The Herald*, a Home-Start spokesperson said:

> '*Struggling to cope with your children isn't something that many people feel able to be open and honest about – parents are under pressure to be perfect. Instagram, Facebook and*

other social media platforms portray a rose-tinted version of reality, often painting unachievable levels of perfect parenting. Parents are fighting to live up to this image rather than feeling able to look for help when life gets too much. Not asking for help when it's needed most can make a difficult situation worse.'

According to Tracey Wade, a psychology professor at Flinders University, there are two components to perfectionism. The first is having high standards. The other is being excessively self-critical, and, when taken to extremes, this can cause problems. Speaking to *The Advertiser* in 2017, Ms Wade said you may '*start comparing yourself to all those images of happy, joyful people on holidays, all those people happily sweaty from their latest workouts, those in what seem to be the most loving relationships, in the cleanest houses, with the most well-pruned gardens, with the most expensive cars in their garages, which drive them to their fulfilling jobs and then come home again to their endlessly cherubic children.'*

Life appears flawless in these images, but the reality is often far from perfect. This can create a sense of inadequacy, as people feel their life is not as good as others'. To make matters worse, many people have become addicted to their smartphones and the social media platforms they support, obsessing over the number of likes or views of their posts. According to a 2018 blog post by Science in the News, or SITN (which features the work of science PhD students at Harvard University), social media platforms '*leverage the very same neural circuitry used by slot machines and cocaine to keep us using their products as much as possible.'*

According to the post, adults in the US spend an average of two to four hours per day tapping, typing and swiping on their devices. There is nothing inherently addictive about smartphones themselves. The article states, '*The true drivers of our attachments to these devices are the hyper-social environments they provide... but their cost is becoming more and more apparent. Studies are beginning to show links between smartphone usage and increased levels of anxiety and depression, poor sleep quality, and increased risk of car injury or death.'*

So, why are smartphones – and, by extension, social media platforms – so hard to ignore?

It all comes down to dopamine – a chemical produced by your brain that plays a major role in motivating your behaviour. It is released when you take a bite of delicious food, have sex, complete a workout and have successful social interactions. In essence, dopamine rewards you for beneficial behaviours and motivates you to repeat them. Cognitive neuroscientists have shown that rewarding social stimuli – likes, comments, laughing faces – activate the dopaminergic reward pathways.

Smartphones provide an unlimited supply of social stimuli, leading to a dopamine influx. As humans, if we perceive a potential reward to be delivered at random – a like, comment or emoji – and if the cost of checking this is minimal, like looking at your smartphone, we will end up habitually checking.

According to the SITN post, one of the ways to overcome this is to disable notifications for social media apps. I have gone beyond this and have only text messages enabled on my device. My wife encourages me to leave my phone at home on occasion, so I can be present with her and the family. In other words, I am focused on generating that 'dopamine influx' through face-to-face interactions with the people I love, rather than people I follow on social media!

The plight of working dads in the 21st century

*'One father is more than a
hundred schoolmasters.'*

– George Herbert

David: There are numerous sources – including UNICEF and the World Economic Forum – indicating that Dutch children are the happiest in the world. According to a 2019 article by CNBC, this is partly due to shorter workweeks, allowing fathers in particular to have more time at home and a higher level of involvement in parenting duties. Other studies suggest Dutch children's relationships with their fathers have improved significantly in line with the increased time they spend together.

The article states that you are just as likely to see a Dutch father pushing a pram or wearing a baby carrier as you would a Dutch mum. And when a child is unwell, the mother and father take turns staying at home, *'with most employers showing understanding and leniency.'*

When I was growing up in Perth, our neighbours were Dutch, the children very similar ages to my sister and me. These neighbours remain very close family friends today – we moved away from Perth in the 1980s and have managed to stay in contact with them. When I am in Perth, I always try and find time to visit them; their mum is like an aunty to me. When I reflect on being a part of their life, I realise they always managed to find the time to work *and* live. Work is not their life, like it has been for me on occasion.

Many years ago, the Netherlands workweek was reduced to thirty-six hours in a bid to combat unemployment. The government compensated those who had been working a forty-hour, nine-to-five workweek by giving them extra time off – either half a day per week or a full day per fortnight. Many Dutch fathers began using this time as their 'papadag', which literally translates to 'daddy day'. Taking a papadag has since become the norm. In 2016, nearly half of young fathers in the Netherlands said they take a day off at least once a week to be at home. That percentage has only continued to increase.

In contrast, a Talking Talent report (based on a survey of more than 8,000 working parents in the UK, the US, Switzerland, Hong Kong, Singapore, China, India and Australia) reveals fifty-eight per cent of working dads often feel guilty that they don't spend enough time with their children. I was one of those dads when I held a particular role. The report also found seventy-five per cent of working dads agree that fathers of this generation want more involvement in their children's care and upbringing than previous generations.

Despite this, Australian dads are not taking more time off work. An Australian Institute of Family Studies report, titled 'Fathers and Work', shows that employment for men with children has been remarkably steady since 1991. The report states, '*In Australia, fathers may request to work part-time hours, as a flexible work option, to assist in the care of children. However, they rarely do.*' Of course, there are options beyond part-time work. For example, some fathers could take advantage of flexible working arrangements, although many do not. Fathers may also be able to take extended time off work after having children, like mothers often do, but data shows they often do not do this either. Why?

According to the Talking Talent report, thirty-nine per cent of working dads agree that those who take extended parental leave find it has a detrimental effect on their career, while forty-three per cent say that fathers who take extended parental leave experience unfavourable comments, discrimination or judgement. Adding to the problem is the fact that fathers are generally not entitled to the same paid parental leave benefits as mothers; fifty-six per cent of dads would be 'very likely' to share extended parental leave if pay and other conditions had met their needs. The report states:

'Too often, beyond a congratulatory handshake, we forget to include working fathers in the conversation at all...Strategic-thinking organisations need to be proactive about promoting paid parental leave and offering equal paid entitlements to both mums and dads. It encourages shared parental responsibility.'

But according to a 2019 article by HRM, a website and magazine owned by the Australian HR Institute, workplace changes *'aren't enough to tip the balance'*:

'Because if a lot of men want to take time off work and aren't afraid to do so, why don't they? The answer might be our society has a particular view of childcare that we tend to follow without much regard for our individual desires. We don't judge others, but nor do we want to be the other.

'How do you broach it with your partner, family and friends? Who wants to be the one father who isn't getting promotions? Or the one mother who isn't across every detail of their child's upbringing? It's hard to bite the bullet and be different.'

Based on my observations and experience, I believe society still deems it more acceptable for women – rather than men – to work part-time (or not at all). When parents choose to undertake child-caring responsibilities, rather than placing their children in childcare, it is generally the woman who does the caring. Within our family, since I have been able to be more flexible with my working hours, my wife has been able to grow her career. The downside is that it was only possible when I stepped away from professional employment.

A couple of years back, I was speaking to a potential Australian client. He was a senior executive at a well-known company, yet sadly appeared overweight, was red-faced and looked unhealthy. When he asked about my life and what I was currently focused on, I explained the balance between work, family and regular exercise. His response was, 'Jeez, it sounds like you have gone a little soft.' These sorts of comments help to explain why some men might be reluctant to pull back from work and spend more time at home. Many men I speak to about this would like greater flexibility. But for whatever reason, they feel they will be judged and labelled as not taking their career seriously.

Woman, interrupted

'Like their personal lives, women's history is fragmented, interrupted; a shadow history of human beings whose existence has been shaped by the efforts and the demands of others.'

– Elizabeth Janeway

David: My wife gives, and has given, more than she has received in her lifetime. As an emergency nurse, she ensures that all her patients receive the greatest level of care possible. She has role modelled this for our children, always taking on more than me in the home. I am worried that my lack of role modelling within the home has set an expectation for my daughters that their role will be like my wife's, if they choose to have a family. As I wrote earlier, I did not learn how to properly cook until well into my forties.

In 2019, Brigid Schulte, an award-winning journalist and author of the book *Overwhelmed*, wrote an article *for The Guardian* titled 'A woman's greatest enemy? A lack of time to herself'. She refers to various women throughout history – including the wives of Sigmund Freud and Karl Marx – who ensured their husbands were given every opportunity to create.

She also highlights women like Patti Scialfa – wife of Bruce Springsteen – who has said how difficult it was to write the music for her solo album as she was constantly interrupted by her children, in a way that Bruce would never have been. As Schulte points out, it is not that women haven't had the talent to make their creative mark. They have just never had the time.

When I was writing my first book, my wife and I agreed that I would collect the children from school, cook meals and take on a portion of the responsibilities that she has undertaken for years. But after several weeks, I was disheartened with my writing progress. After chatting with her about this, we agreed that I could relinquish some of these tasks in order to crack on with the writing. It worked.

Throughout history, women have had their time interrupted. Even today, women still spend at least twice as much time as men doing household work and caring for children – sometimes much more. During COVID-19, it quickly became evident that mums, rather than dads, were undertaking the vast majority of their children's home schooling.

Even at work, a study of male and female professors reveals women's time is more interrupted and fragmented than men's, as women shoulder more service work, mentoring and teaching. In contrast, says Schulte, '*men spent more of their work days in long stretches of uninterrupted time to think, research, write, create and publish to make their names, advance their careers and get their ideas out into the world.*'

Melinda Gates laments the constant state of interruption in her book *The Moment of Lift*:

> *'I've been trying to carve out time to think and write...Every single time I've sat down to start, I've gotten a panicked call or email from my husband, son or daughter; my mother, dealing with the strange frontier and endless paperwork of the newly widowed; a credit card company; or a mechanic about some emergency or other that requires my immediate attention to stave off certain disaster.'*

A key message from Melinda Gates, at her London book launch in 2019, was that small behavioural changes can really make a difference, and more role modelling from women can really show people – men and women – what is possible.

When I reflect upon the birth of our children, my wife was keen to continue working. When our second daughter was only months old, my wife worked for a health start-up out of our apartment in London and continued her hospital risk management job two days a week. This required compromise from both of us – she was often exhausted, and we had less time together – but it has had multiple benefits. Her stories as a risk manager, auditor and nurse are a source of intrigue for our children. They are proud of the professional work she does, and it sets an example of what is possible. By keeping her nursing registration active, through the odd shift, she has been able to step in and out of work to suit our growing family. We are fortunate that nursing offers this flexibility.

However, not all women have had this experience. I know many Gen-X mothers have been unable to continue their careers, as they did not want their children in full-time childcare, and their partner wasn't willing or able to reduce his work hours.

Brigid Schulte sums it up well in her article with a reference to Virginia Woolf, who once imagined what would have become of

William Shakespeare had he been female, or if he'd had an equally gifted sister:

> 'The female Shakespeare, Woolf wrote, would never have had the time or the ability to develop her genius...But that wasn't the end of the story. Woolf imagined that, in the future, a woman with genius would be born. Her ability to blossom – and the expectation that her voice, her vision, was worthy – would depend entirely on the world we decided to create. "She would come if we worked for her," Woolf wrote.'

Gen X is sandwiched and feeling the squeeze

'I am a member of the "sandwich" generation, that group that must simultaneously care for elderly parents and support children.'

– Sandra Tsing Loh

David: I am unable to recall how my parents cared for my grandparents, and to what extent, but I do vaguely recall an uncle and aunty caring for them. (For any family members reading this book, I am not diminishing any effort made. I just don't remember, as I was young at the time and I may have been daydreaming.)

Today, the situation is very demanding for many people my age. Many of them are working and looking after children and, increasingly, caring for ageing parents. My wife knows firsthand how difficult it is, having cared for her mother while also raising our three children and supporting me in my career, which often required me to work away regularly.

We are not alone. According to a 2019 report released by the US-based National Alliance for Caregiving (NAC) and Caring Across Generations, Generation X is the largest group of sandwich caregivers in the US, comprising nearly half (forty-nine per cent) of all sandwich caregivers. The report reveals fifty-nine per cent of Gen X are caring for a parent or parent-in-law, while fourteen per cent are caring for a neighbour. On average, Gen X caregivers have been providing care for 3.4 years. The report states:

'Most Gen X sandwich caregivers are the primary caregiver for their recipient (61 percent) and provide 22.6 hours of care weekly.

'...Most Gen X sandwich caregivers reported having worked in the past year while providing care (64 percent), working 36.4 hours a week on average. These Gen X sandwich caregivers have experienced negative work impacts more often as a result of their caregiving role (65 percent vs. 46 percent of baby boomer sandwich caregivers), including 26 percent who took a leave of absence to provide care. Perhaps due to these work impacts, 25 percent of Gen X sandwich caregivers reported high levels of financial strain as a result of caregiving (compared to 12 percent for baby boomers).'

The care of our elderly will be even more demanding for future generations. Often, this care falls to women; it has on both sides of my family to date. That is not a coincidence, either. A study published in 2019 in *The Journals of Gerontology* (published by Oxford University Press) found women experience a greater caregiving burden than men. They are seventy-three per cent more likely to leave the labour market and twice as likely to take time off due to informal care.

A separate study in the US shows most caregivers (sixty-two per cent) are still female. Where higher-hour care is required, sixty-two per cent of women provide more than twenty hours of care per week, compared to thirty-eight per cent of men. Among other things, this can lead to 'caregiver burnout', whereby caregivers experience an '*all-encompassing type of exhaustion when they strive to do more than they are realistically capable of.*'

Ada Calhoun touches on this in her book, *Why We Can't Sleep: Women's New Midlife Crisis*, which highlights the midlife realities faced by Gen X women:

> '*Gen X has arrived in middle age to almost no notice, and largely unaware of being a uniquely star-crossed cohort. "Gen Xers are in 'the prime of their lives' at a particularly divisive and dangerous moment," author and marketing expert Faith Popcorn told me. "They have been hit hard financially and dismissed culturally. They have tons of debt. They're squeezed on both sides, by children and ageing parents. The grim state of adulthood is hitting them hard. If they're exhausted and bewildered, they have every reason to feel that way."*'

The sandwich generation is all of us

'First we are children to our parents, then parents to our children, then parents to our parents, then children to our children.'

– Milton Greenblatt

Michelle: While I can appreciate the extent to which Gen X is being sandwiched, Gen Y is facing the same fate, if not worse. The same report referenced by David in the previous section (from the NAC and Caring Across Generations) shows thirty-one per cent of sandwich caregivers are Gen Y. More than a third (thirty-three per cent) care for a parent, twenty-three per cent a grandparent, and sixteen per cent a friend or neighbour. On average, Gen Y sandwich caregivers have been providing care for 2.1 years, providing an average of 17.3 hours of care per week.

But here is the kicker: The majority (seventy-six per cent) of Gen Y sandwich caregivers work while providing care, but fewer report having workplace benefits like flexible work hours (forty-four per cent), paid sick days (thirty-one per cent) or employee support programs (thirteen per cent). The report features commentary from Dr Feylyn Lewis, a research fellow at the University of Sussex, whose research involves the mental health needs of young caregivers in multiple countries. According to Dr Lewis, it is important to draw attention to the specific issues facing this group:

> *'This report highlights that millennial sandwich caregivers are more likely to engage in paid employment in comparison to other age groups of sandwich caregivers, but they are the least likely to have supportive workplace policies. Recalling that millennials may be at the beginning stages of their career, they may be in a more insecure employment position than older generations of sandwich caregivers.*

> *'...Beyond paid leave policies, millennial sandwich caregivers would benefit from flexible working hours, a more empathetic workplace culture, and depending upon their job sector, the ability to telecommute.'*

I know firsthand how challenging it is to juggle full-time study and, later, full-time work while also being a Gen Y caregiver (and now, with the birth of my own child, a Gen Y *sandwich* caregiver). My father was diagnosed with Parkinson's disease when I was a teenager. From the age of eighteen, I have cared for him in various capacities. Initially, this involved driving him to appointments, running errands on his behalf and helping with housework (he lived alone). But as his condition worsened, his reliance on me grew. Even after moving to Melbourne, I would often have to leave my desk to field calls from specialists, nurses and so on. While I was lucky to work in supportive environments, I always felt a bit guilty if I needed to take a call.

My dad has since moved to a nursing home, where he receives the level of care he needs. However, I still help him with more personal errands and tasks, such as taking him to the bank, assisting with paperwork and so on. Now that I work from home, it is *much* easier for me to take calls and help my father as and when he needs it. However, I am well aware that not every sandwich caregiver is in my position. As people continue to live longer, and flexible work increasingly becomes the norm, I believe companies will start to rethink how they approach their employees' caregiving responsibilities – just as they have done with regard to parental leave.

And to help ease the pressure of being 'squeezed' – by caring for children in addition to ageing parents – we will see a rise in multigenerational housing. In fact, research suggests one in five Australians already live in a multigenerational household – and that number appears to be increasing. According to Dr Edgar Liu from the University of New South Wales, much of the increase is being driven by a desire for baby boomers to stay living at home, rather than move into residential aged care.

It also means that, where possible, grandparents can help with raising children. In fact, a University of Oxford research paper, titled 'Twenty-first century grandparents: global perspectives on changing roles and consequences', indicates many grandparents are already filling the 'parenting gap', particularly in single-parent households, by attending school meetings, helping with homework and so on. The paper states, '*There is now a growing body of research that illustrates that grandparent involvement is associated with improved mental health, improved resilience and pro-social behaviour in grandchildren.*' I am not sure a multigenerational household is the option I'd choose, but I can see why many people are attracted to it and why it will become increasingly popular. After all, multigenerational families are a common way of life in many other parts of the world.

Three generations, three parenting styles

'The rules of parenting have changed.
By the modern definition, we were a
generation of neglected children.'

– Richard Linklater

David: When I was growing up, my dad often travelled for work, and so I only saw him in the evening. My children have so far experienced a different type of dad. Until my eldest daughter went to school, she was accustomed to me working a day or two per week out of our apartment in London. As a result, she has an incredible ability to sense when I am on a call or video conference and intuitively knows when and how to be quiet. (This will serve her future housemates and/or partner well!) She has role modelled this for our other children, who have followed suit. (Well, most of the time!)

We relocated from London to Melbourne when our eldest daughter was about to commence school. It was a tough move for me, leaving a job and colleagues I loved. However, the benefits for our family have made the move worth it. When I started working again in Australia, I was dressed in a suit one morning and walked out to say goodbye to my eldest daughter. She asked me, 'Are you going to a wedding?' It was so foreign for her to see me suited up for work, as she was used to seeing me in jeans, a shirt and a jumper. It made me realise how different I was to my own father, who would never have dressed so casually for work.

And it made me wonder: How do millennial parents differ again?

According to a 2017 article by *Business Insider* (which draws statistics from a range of sources), millennial parents, nicknamed 'parennials', are raising their children differently to previous generations – in many different ways. For example, they are more likely to seek parenting advice online, with a *New York Times* article stating, '*Google is the new grandparent, the new neighbour, the new nanny.*'

Parennials are also more likely to document their children's lives on social media, with some giving their kids personal hashtags and YouTube channels. Ironically, a poll conducted by *Time* and SurveyMonkey found almost a fifth (nineteen per cent) of parennials have never shared a photo of their children on social media, compared to thirty per cent of Gen X parents and fifty-three per cent of baby boomer parents.

A separate survey, conducted by OnePoll on behalf of GoDaddy, found twenty per cent of parennials said they changed or considered changing their baby's name based on available domain names. (I must admit I checked available domains for my own children when I wrote my first book – although I would not go so far as to change their names!)

According to a Pew Research Center survey, fifty-seven per cent of millennial mums and forty-three per cent of millennial dads believe they are doing a very good job as a parent. In contrast, forty-eight per cent of Gen X mums and just thirty-seven per cent of Gen X dads said the same. Like many parents (Gen Y and Gen X alike), my biggest challenge is time – the time I have available and the time I need to dedicate to things. In some ways, I would rate myself poorly in this regard, not only as a father but as a husband, son, brother, cousin, uncle and friend.

Parennials may have more confidence in their parenting skills, but the research shows they are more likely to struggle financially – thanks to the increasing cost of childcare and education, stagnant wages and student loan debt. In fact, according to a 2015 article in *The Washington Post*, the average eighteen- to thirty-four-year-old is making $2,000 *less* than they would have in 1980. This makes me wonder what the future will be like for my children when they themselves become parents.

Parennials also spend more time with their children than previous generations. A 2016 study, published in the Journal of Marriage and Family, found that mothers from eleven wealthy Western countries spend about an hour more per day taking care of their children than mothers did in 1965. Dads are also spending more time looking after their children – almost an hour, up from an average of just sixteen minutes in 1965.

The dilemma of falling fertility rates

'The ageing and declining population will have far-reaching impacts. Declining fertility rates will possibly increase immigration. The structure of family and society will inevitably change.'

– Toshihiko Fukui

Michelle: In the previous section, David highlighted some of the ways in which millennials are doing things differently when it comes to parenting. But there is another, far bigger trend sweeping the world: falling fertility rates.

According to a 2020 BBC article, which references a study published in *The Lancet*, the global total fertility rate (TFR) nearly halved to 2.4 in 2017 (compared to 4.7 in 1950). The study was conducted by researchers at the Institute for Health Metrics and Evaluation at the University of Washington. It shows the global TFR is projected to fall to 1.66 by 2100. As a result, the researchers expect the number of people on the planet to peak at 9.73 billion in 2064 before falling to 8.79 billion by the end of the century. They go on to say:

> *'By 2050, 151 countries were forecasted to have a TFR lower than the replacement level (TFR <2.1), and 183 were forecasted to have a TFR lower than replacement by 2100. 23 countries in the reference scenario, including Japan, Thailand, and Spain, were forecasted to have population declines greater than 50% from 2017 to 2100.'*

From an environmental perspective, a declining population is undoubtedly a good thing. But consider this: *'Findings also suggest a shifting age structure in many parts of the world, with 2.37 billion (1.91–2.87) individuals older than 65 years and 1.70 billion (1.11– 2.81) individuals younger than 20 years, forecasted globally in 2100.'* Specifically, the number of children aged under five will fall from 681 million in 2017 to 401 million in 2100, while the number of adults aged over eighty will soar from 141 million in 2017 to a whopping 866 million in 2100.

According to researcher Professor Christopher Murray, this will create 'enormous social change', as there will be fewer and fewer taxpayers to support an increasingly ageing population. Some countries, including the United Kingdom, have used migration to boost their population and compensate for falling fertility rates. Other countries have actively tried to boost fertility rates with policies such as enhanced maternity and paternity leave, free childcare, financial incentives and extra employment rights. Sweden has managed to drag its fertility rate up from 1.7 to 1.9, but other countries have struggled.

In 2002, the Australian government introduced the Baby Bonus, which saw new parents receive tax cuts and, later, lump-sum payments for each eligible child. At the time, then Treasurer Peter Costello did not mince his words when he said young Australian couples should *have one for mum, one for dad and one for the country.*

But according to the Australian Bureau of Statistics, the number of couples without children will eventually overtake the number of couples *with* children – suggesting Peter Costello's plea is largely falling on deaf ears.

Nevertheless, his words were echoed in 2020 when sitting Treasurer Josh Frydenberg made a plea to Australians to have more children – if for no other reason than to help grow the population and economy in the wake of COVID-19 and the subsequent closure of international borders, which had halved Australia's population growth. In a speech to the National Press Club, Mr Frydenberg said population growth was expected to slow to 0.6 per cent in 2021 – the lowest rate since 1916-17.

> *'I can say that people should feel encouraged about the future and the more children that we have across the country, together with our migration, we will build our population growth and that will be good for the economy,' he said. 'I think the best thing we can do to encourage more children being born across the country is obviously to create a strong economy for them to be born into.'*

But is it really as simple as that? Could it be that people are having fewer children – or no children at all – by choice? In many parts of the world, women now have complete control over their own lives (as they should). For many women – particularly those with rewarding careers, busy social lives and a desire to travel – that doesn't include having a baby.

Some people are choosing not to have children for environmental reasons, which has led to campaigns such as BirthStrike – a worldwide movement of people who refuse to have children due to climate change. Even women who are mothers may decide against having another child because of existing family responsibilities, like ageing parents. As David and I have already highlighted, many women are buckling under the pressure that comes with being 'sandwiched', so why add to it by having more children?

A 2002 study, titled 'Regret and Psychological Well-Being among Voluntarily and Involuntarily Childless Women and Mothers', found that voluntarily childless women show higher levels of overall wellbeing, rate themselves as more autonomous within their environment and are less likely to have a child-related regret. The study revealed that about a third of women categorised by researchers as involuntarily childless indicate they are in fact 'childless by choice'. These women report making an active decision to accept the childless lifestyle and focus on the future, thus exerting control over their situation.

I am fairly sure that I only want one child. This decision has nothing to do with 'the economy' or finances. Honestly, I do not see a compelling enough reason to have a second child. My husband and I want to experience parenthood, but we also want to maintain some semblance of our current lifestyle. I also happen to love the work that I do. If I have more than one child, that means more time away from my work.

So, while I understand and appreciate the concern regarding falling fertility rates, I do not see a clear way to address this.

Reflection

David: Chapter 7 began with a focus on Gen Y and the notion of the quarter-life crisis. Will Gen Z face the same struggles? From there, we turned our focus to the myth of the perfect parent – a myth being perpetuated by the pervasive and addictive nature of social media. I highlighted the plight of modern-day working dads and the concept of papadag, before exploring some of the struggles facing Gen X – namely, being 'sandwiched' between children and parents. But this problem is not specific to Gen X, as Gen Y is also feeling the squeeze. At the end of the chapter, Michelle highlighted one of the world's biggest yet seemingly unsolvable challenges: falling fertility rates.

When reflecting on this chapter, consider:

- Do you think Gen Z will face the same struggles as Gen Y? Why or why not?
- Do you feel pressure to be the perfect parent? Does social media exacerbate this?
- Do you turn off your social media notifications? Do you know someone who should?
- What do you think of the idea of working dads taking a regular papadag (daddy day)?
- Do you agree with the claim that women's time is routinely interrupted more than men's? How does this affect you?
- If you're a member of Gen X or Gen Y, are you sandwiched between caregiving for parents and children? How does this affect you?
- Do you have a particular parenting style? How does it differ to your own parents' style?
- What are your thoughts on falling fertility rates? Do you think there's a way to address this?

CHAPTER 8

We Are Australian

*'Australia is about as far away
as you can get. I like that.'*

– Andre Benjamin

Michelle: In this final chapter, David starts by highlighting the changing nature of Australian families. Later in the chapter, he draws attention to the way in which elderly people are treated, suggesting Australians would do well to emulate some of the cultural attitudes adopted in other countries. Meanwhile, I discuss the pursuit of work-life balance as it applies to Australian women, before touching on some of the challenges that come with being an Australian member of Gen Y. I also explore the ideas of multigenerational living and solo households – both of which are set to rise in this country.

The changing makeup of Australian families

*'The family is changing, not disappearing.
We have to broaden our understanding
of it, look for the new metaphors.'*

– Mary Catherine Bateson

David: Within Australia, based on the 2016 Census, the most common family form is a couple family with no children (37.76 per cent), followed by a couple family with dependent children under the age of fifteen (30.64 per cent). One-parent families with dependent children comprise around eight per cent of all Australian families.

The 2016 Census also found more blended families, as couples dissolve (due to separation, divorce or death of a partner) and new families are formed. Blended families account for 3.7 per cent of families. This includes families with two or more children, at least one of whom is the natural or adopted child of both partners and at least one other child who is the stepchild of one of them. A further sixty-three per cent of families are stepfamilies, which have at least one resident stepchild, but no child who is the natural or adopted child of both partners. Michelle and I are both part of stepfamilies.

In fact, I have been a member of a traditional family (until the age of six), a one-parent family (for several years after my mother died) and a stepfamily. When growing up, I found the latter two the more challenging. Everyone tried their best. However, when you're in a family with your own 'flesh and blood', I believe there is a higher level of intuition and understanding.

I am not alone in this perspective; others with similar experiences have shared similar observations with me. I was, therefore, pleased to discover within our research the emergence of more grandparent-led families. Grandparent-led families have increased from an estimated 22,500 in 2004 to 60,000 in 2016. More than half (fifty-three per cent) of grandparent families are couple families with grandchildren and forty-seven per cent are lone grandparent families.

There's also a rise in the number of young adults living at home with their parents, as Michelle and I have both touched on several times already. According to the Australian Institute of Family Studies (AIFS), forty-three per cent of those aged twenty to twenty-four were living in the family home in 2016, up from thirty-six per cent in 1981. The number of adults aged twenty-five to twenty-nine still at home has also increased – from ten per cent in 1981 to seventeen per cent in 2016.

'A range of factors, including the cost of housing in capital cities and time spent in higher education, have contributed to a growing trend for more young people to delay moving out in recent decades,' said AIFS director Anne Hollonds.

Interestingly, an increasingly higher proportion of young women are living with their parents. AIFS researcher Lixia Qu said:

'Our analysis shows that 47% of 20–24-year-old men were living in the family home in 2016, compared to 39% of young women in that age group. However, the proportion of young women opting to live with parents is growing at a faster rate than that for young men.

'The percentage of young men living at home only increased slightly between 1981 and 2016, while the proportion of young women living with their parents rose from 27% in 1981 to 39% in 2016....one of the factors is likely to be that fewer of today's young women leave the family home to get married as was once more common.'

Even though the Australian population has doubled since the early 1970s, there were fewer marriages in 2017 than in 1970 (112,954 compared to 116,066). In 2017, the rate was 4.6 marriages per 1,000 Australian residents – the lowest rate ever recorded. And since 1976, Australia's birth rate has been below the replacement level. In 2017, the total fertility rate was 1.74, declining from a peak of 3.55 in 1961. But as Michelle highlighted in Chapter 7, a falling fertility rate is not a problem exclusive to Australia. And there is no clear solution, either.

In a 2018 SBS article, Brendan Churchill, Convenor of The Australian Sociological Association's (TASA) Families and Relationships Thematic Group, said the image of the typical family – mum, dad and two kids – is fading as Australian families become increasingly diverse:

> *'While the idealised nuclear family of the past is no more, this does not mean that the family as a social institution is in decline, or that families in contemporary Australia are at risk. But it does mean families are changing. Our political leaders should reflect on this diversity to ensure social policies reflect these differences, so that all families are well supported.'*

Australian women and the pursuit of work-life balance

> *'To have someone who never makes a mistake, never finds her personal life in disarray, never worries about work-life balance? I think that would be unreal.'*
>
> **– Sophie Kinsella**

Michelle: In Chapter 6, David referenced an article by Brigid Schulte, who wrote: '[Virginia] *Woolf imagined that, in the future, a woman with genius would be born. Her ability to blossom – and the expectation that her voice, her vision, was worthy – would depend entirely on the world we decided to create. "She would come if we worked for her," Woolf wrote.'*

Now, almost a century later, I must ask: Have we worked hard enough for women to blossom?

It is still a work in progress, I'd say, although there's no doubt we've come a long way since the time of Virginia Woolf – and certainly since the time of Shakespeare (whom Woolf's comments were inspired by). Gender equality and women's empowerment is now a shared goal in many different parts of the world – as seen by the rise of International Women's Day.

International Women's Day is a global celebration of the social, economic, cultural and political achievements of women. But with many women now wearing a multitude of different hats for different roles, is it still possible for them to achieve a healthy work-life balance?

An Australian Institute of Health and Welfare report found Australia ranked twenty-seven out of thirty-five OECD countries when it comes to work-life balance. The Australian Work and Life Index shows certain groups are more affected than others by an imbalance in work and personal time, including:

- Women who typically have less adequate work-life balance than men, and do around twice as much caring and domestic work on average
- Parents, particularly mothers (single mothers even more so)
- People who are caring for others, such as sick, elderly or disabled relatives
- The 'sandwich generation' – typically women who care for children as well as elderly or sick relatives

According to Melinda Tyro, Enterprise Sales Manager at resume service CVCheck, women tend to put too much pressure on themselves. In a 2020 company article, she said, '*Women...rarely say that their life is their own; instead, our life is segmented, with each segment belonging to other people. It belongs to our children, our partners, our friends, and our employers.'*

The same article states that in 2019, three different research papers revealed:

- Roughly two-thirds of women aged under thirty-six reported feeling nervous, anxious or on edge. One in three had these feelings nearly every day.
- Two-thirds of surveyed mothers were considering leaving their job within twelve months of commencing a new role due to stress caused by the conflict between work and caring.
- Increasing numbers of young women are deciding not to have children because they are discouraged by the lack of work-life balance demonstrated by working mothers around them.

The work-life juggle can severely impact family life. According to the 2019 National Working Families Report, two-thirds of working parents reported feeling too emotionally or physically drained when they got home from work to contribute to their family. Half of all women and a third of men who were parenting or caring said they were under 'a lot' of stress or 'a great deal' of stress. A third said the combination of work and family responsibilities contributed to stress and tension in their relationships with their partner and children, while half had missed out on family activities in the past month due to time they had to spend at work.

Women's careers can also be affected by the work-life balance pursuit. According to CVCheck, there can be a temptation to plan a career path around jobs that will offer the most flexibility rather than the best opportunities or the most fulfilment. The article states, *'Women seeking work-life balance will often track sideways or sit for years in jobs that are flexible rather than pursuing opportunities for promotion.'*

Meanwhile, a 2017 article in the *Chicago Tribune* reveals that many women, particularly those in high-powered executive roles, are often wary of discussing their children at work, fearing it would look 'weak' to remind bosses of commitments outside of the office. The article encourages women (and men) to share details of their family life – if they want to – because '*a personal life is something to prize, not hide.*'

In a 2019 article for *The Sydney Morning Herald*, full-time worker and mum-of-two Mia Greves said she knew 'something had to give'. With the support of her employer, Ms Greves dropped half a day to spend Friday afternoons with her children – and has found the shift life-enhancing. '*It's made a huge difference to our family dynamic, that Friday afternoon...*[My children] *get all of me. I am present and I enjoy it,*' she said.

So, what can employers do to help women and men achieve greater work-life balance? One of the suggestions put forward by CVCheck is to avoid creating a culture of 'everything is urgent', as this allows employees to truly switch off at the end of their workday.

The pleasure and pain of being Gen Y

'Millennials get a bad rap sometimes about their grit and perseverance.'

– Andrew Yang

Michelle: In July 2020, Australian media legend Ita Buttrose made headlines when she said millennial workers lack resilience and 'need hugging'. Speaking to the Australia-United Kingdom Chamber of Commerce in London, Buttrose said the makeup of the workforce had changed radically, particularly the demands of millennials. As reported by *The Sydney Morning Herald*:

> '[Millennial workers] *need much more reassurance and they need to be thanked, which is something many companies don't do. They're very keen on being thanked and they almost need hugging...they seem to lack the resilience that I remember from my younger days.*'

She said resilience seemed to be in 'short supply' worldwide, suggesting 'bad parenting' may be to blame. According to Buttrose, resilience is '*something we need to foster in everybody from a very young age*'. Not surprisingly, her comments hit a nerve among Gen Y workers – particularly in light of COVID-19, which has left millions of people across the world unemployed. This is particularly distressing when you consider that Gen Y likely made up fifty per cent of the global workforce in 2020, according to PwC.

Even those who have managed to hold on to their jobs are on shaky ground, in many cases. According to a report titled 'Gen Y on Gen Y' (part of the University of Melbourne's Life Patterns research program, which I first referenced in Chapter 2), Gen Y is the most educated Australian generation yet. In fact, twenty-one per cent have returned to study after completing an undergraduate degree.

But it takes a long time to pay off. In their late twenties, less than three-quarters of Gen Y are in full-time work. Many of those who are employed have yet to find work in their area of study. In 2017, twenty-three per cent of men and twenty-seven per cent of women aged twenty-eight to twenty-nine were on limited-term, renewable or casual contracts. Almost half (forty-four per cent) were working nights or evening shifts, while fifty-nine per cent worked on weekends. And according to the Australia Institute, workers in their early and mid career do the most unpaid overtime

– 7.85 hours a week for those aged twenty-five to thirty-four and 7.4 hours a week for those aged thirty-five to forty-four.

As highlighted in Chapter 2, one of Gen Y's biggest concerns is cost of living (second only to the environment). This worry isn't imagined, either. According to the US-based Pew Research Center, millennials have less wealth than baby boomers did at the same age. In 2016, the median net worth of households headed by millennials was about $12,500. At the same age, households headed by boomers had a median net worth of $20,700.

A 2019 Grattan Institute report, titled 'Generation gap: Ensuring a fair go for younger Australians', reveals the wealth of households under thirty-five has barely moved since 2004. Millennials – many of whom started their careers in the wake of the global financial crisis – have also been somewhat slower in forming their own households than previous generations. According to the Pew Research Center, millennials are more likely to live in their parents' home and also more likely to be at home for longer stretches. In 2018, fifteen per cent of millennials were living with their parents. This is nearly double the share of early baby boomers (eight per cent).

The Grattan Institute report is quick to quash the theory that millennials do not know how to save, stating:

> *'There is no evidence that young people's spending habits are to blame for their stagnating wealth – this is not a problem caused by avocado brunches or too many lattes. In fact, younger people are spending less on non-essential items such as alcohol, clothing and personal care, and more on necessities such as housing, than three decades ago.'*

The report goes on to highlight the unique financial pressures on younger people, stating, '*If low wage growth and fewer working hours is the "new normal", then we could have a generation emerge from young adulthood with lower incomes than the one before it. This has already happened in the US and UK.'*

I was born in 1987 and graduated from university in 2008 – when the GFC was in full force. As a journalism graduate, I was one of the lucky few who actually landed a job in the industry straight off the bat. The catch? I had to move from Perth to Port Hedland, a dusty mining town in the north of Western Australia. I went willingly, despite an appallingly low salary.

After eighteen months, I moved to Melbourne, where I furthered my career in journalism (on another lowly salary) before eventually moving into editing. For three years, I commuted from the outer suburbs into the CBD every single weekday. The commute took an hour each way, and I had an eye-watering start time of 7:30am. I was up at 5:30am and did not arrive home until 6:30pm at the earliest. I left the house in the dark and arrived home in the dark.

I turned thirty in 2017. By this stage, it was not uncommon for people my age to have a 'side hustle' as a way of making extra money. Even those on full-time salaries – including myself – pursued various forms of casual or freelance work in order to 'get ahead'. But for many members of Gen Y, getting ahead is just a fanciful idea. For many, simply staying afloat has become a more reasonable life goal.

So, do I agree that Gen Y lacks resilience? Absolutely not. Could most of us do with a hug? Undoubtedly. And while the 'she'll be right' sentiment may have resonated with Ita's generation, it seems outdated and even somewhat damaging now. On the contrary, what we need is action.

The Grattan Institute report outlines several recommendations, including changes to planning rules to encourage higher-density living in established city suburbs, which would make housing more affordable, and reducing or eliminating age-based tax breaks, which are *'pushing a growing tax burden on to working Australians.'* The report states, *'Just as policy changes have contributed to pressures on young people, they can help redress them. The time for action is now: none of us wants the legacy of a generation left behind.'*

Multigenerational living isn't necessarily a bad thing

'Legacy is not what I did for myself. It's what I'm doing for the next generation.'

– Vitor Belfort

Michelle: As highlighted in the previous section, a higher proportion of young Australians are still living at home. But what are some of the implications – and how can they be addressed?

According to the Australian Unity Wellbeing Index, conducted by Deakin University, adults living at home with their parents aren't doing so well in the happiness stakes. In fact, in 2016, their personal wellbeing dipped to its lowest point in a decade. Those living with their parents also scored the lowest levels of satisfaction for personal relationships, community connectedness and achieving in life.

In a 2019 ABC Everyday article, Rebecca Huntley said there are 'complex structural and societal reasons' why young people are remaining at home longer, stating the 'failure to launch' claim is not only damaging but unfair:

> *'There has been a stigma in some societies associated with remaining at home after the age of consent....But in my view, the negative perceptions associated with adults still living at*

home are unfair to both parents and children. And they are preventing us from finding new and potentially positive ways to create different kinds of living arrangements.'

According to Huntley, we need to improve the structural inequalities in the system that prevent young people from moving out of their parents' home. '*One of the greatest challenges we face as a society is how we can provide housing, care and support for Australians up and down the family tree,*' she says.

Perhaps Australia could take some lessons from Canada. The Millennial Report – authored by the Real Estate Investment Network and aimed at developers and investors – shows how millennials are getting creative about home ownership.

As I touched on in Chapter 7, there is an increasing trend in multigenerational living, whereby a young person will continue living with their parents – even after they have their own partner and young children – and potentially buy into the family home. This is being facilitated by granny flats and the like, as ageing parents move out of the main home to allow for the young person and their growing family to take over the house.

The report states:

'There is an increase in intergenerational living, and it is the Millennials who lead the way in this new trend... it is a coinciding of two significant life-course moments affecting parent and child that has led to an increase of intergenerational households – Millennials cannot afford to buy a home, and baby boomers want to age in place. In this scenario, while both generations may sacrifice, they also both gain.'

We 'manage' our elderly; other countries treasure theirs

'The young man knows the rules, but the old man knows the exceptions.'

– Oliver Wendell Holmes, Sr.

David: A former colleague of mine was born and raised in India. We worked closely together for several years and became good friends; I was always interested in his cultural insights and stories of his childhood. One evening, we were discussing some clear differences between the UK, India and Australia. I had been living in the UK for six or so years by that point. As we were chatting, a television news segment was reporting projections regarding the cost of aged care and the complexity of services required for an ageing population.

My colleague explained that within his culture, the eldest person in the family is regarded as the wisest and most trusted. It is custom for younger generations to touch the feet of their grandparents or elders, show them love and respect, and seek their blessings. Older people receive great care from their families, and their experiences are readily shared for the benefit of other family members. Also, time spent with the elderly is treasured every day.

This is in stark contrast to some Western families, which only come together in someone's last days (or after the person has died). In Western culture, old age is often presented negatively too. For example, you may have heard such expressions as 'old biddies', 'on borrowed time' and 'one foot in the grave'. It is usually said tongue in-cheek, but this type of language reinforces the notion that older people are redundant and have limited value in the family and, more broadly, society. In contrast, some families marvel at what their grandparents and parents can do, and so have great respect for them.

However, elderly abuse remains a problem, with one in ten Americans experiencing it, and sadly one in six globally. An article by GreatSeniorLiving.com defines elder abuse as *'any action or inaction that harms, endangers, or causes distress to a person over the age of 60 or 65 and is done intentionally by someone who is known to the victim and in a position of trust.'*

Yet, in other countries, if the elderly are not protected and cared for, you may even find yourself in trouble with the law. A 2016 *Marie Claire* article reveals that in China, an 'elderly rights law' is designed to ensure adult children never neglect or snub their elderly parents and that they visit them often, regardless of proximity. In Singapore, parents can sue their adult children for an allowance.

I have a Singaporean friend who was approached by their employer for a promotion in Hong Kong. They declined, as it would have hindered their ability to care for their parents-in-law. I doubt any of my Western colleagues would decline a promotion in similar circumstances.

Within Asia more broadly, it is normal for elderly parents to become the responsibility of adult children. In fact, children are brought up in the knowledge that they will eventually swap roles with their parents, becoming their parents' primary carer and protector. According to UCLA professor Jared Diamond, in East Asian culture it is considered 'utterly despicable' not to take care of your adult parents.

Meanwhile, in the Mediterranean, respect for elders operates as a cultural norm and it is common for extended families to live under one roof. Similar setups are evident within African-American families, where grandparents tend to live with families and age is celebrated. Similarly, in Japan, sixtieth and seventieth birthdays are marked as big celebrations.

My wife and I come from two different cultures. Mine is two generations of Australians, with British and Irish heritage. My wife was born in Australia while her parents were born in northern Greece. I love the differences between our cultural backgrounds. My wife's family is very loving and warm, involved in each other's lives, and happy to share their opinions and perspectives very directly with each other.

And within her family, I have seen firsthand how eager the younger generations are to care for elderly family members. My wife's grandparents were cared for by her uncle, for example. Similarly, when my wife's mother reached a certain age, she was moved to within walking distance of our home so that my wife and her sisters could care for her. As the population continues to age, and as multigenerational living becomes increasingly common, I think there is an opportunity for many Australians to reframe the way they think about the elderly – particularly within their own family.

Adapting to the rise of solo households

*'Living alone is as good in its own way.
But we haven't quite given ourselves
permission to recognise that.'*

– Barbara Feldon

Michelle: In 2016, the Australian Bureau of Statistics recorded two million solo households. That number is projected to rise to as many as 3.5 million by 2041, making up twenty-four to twenty-seven per cent of all Australian households.

Whereas in the past, elderly widows were more commonly found to be living alone, we are now increasingly seeing middle-aged adults living alone. In fact, single-male-parent families are projected to increase the fastest of any family type, increasing by forty-four to sixty-five per cent by 2041. Meanwhile, single-female-parent families are projected to make up thirteen to fourteen per cent of all families in 2041 (compared to thirteen per cent in 2016). And while many younger people still live in family households, the number of people aged twenty to twenty-nine living alone has almost doubled in the past thirty years, according to the Department of Social Services.

One of the biggest issues associated with living alone is loneliness, as David and I discussed in Chapter 6. But there are other issues as well. According to CareSearch, older people in particular may struggle with the reality of living alone – particularly if they require care and don't have the support of family and friends:

> 'Those without a caregiver need considerably more practical assistance and liaison regarding care...Some people will move in with family, or others will have relatives helping at home by staying with them overnight as needed.

> 'Others living alone will not have family or close friends, managing sometimes with the help of neighbours or local community resources such as community health services, local councils and the church, or sometimes with no help at all. Some individuals have a strong need to maintain their independence and will often have the resilience to manage by themselves for long periods of time. Some will refuse all offers of help however there are often safety implications in these choices for the health professionals who interact with them.'

In a 2019 article by The Fifth Estate, Georgia Vitale, a researcher at engineering firm Arup, said we need to rethink the way we accommodate the needs of people living alone. For starters, research reveals many solo dwellers still live in big houses – some with as many as three bedrooms. There is a shortage of smaller homes and studios in this country; larger, detached dwellings make up seventy-two per cent of Australia's existing housing stock. According to Vitale, big homes remain *'ingrained in the Australian psyche'*. I'd say this is particularly prevalent among the older generations, as I believe they're more likely to associate big homes with success.

As a result, single people living in large homes are using more resources, including energy for heating and cooling, than they might otherwise use if they lived in smaller homes. Safety is another concern, with the article stating security measures are not enough – people living alone need to *feel* safe:

> *'This is why safe spaces outside a dwelling, where people can interact with friends and neighbours, are critical. It is also more important for people who live alone, who are less likely to own a car, to be safe walking through local streets.'*

Similarly, spaces such as dog parks and community libraries can alleviate feelings of loneliness – particularly among those who are living alone involuntarily, such as after a breakup or the death of a partner. For example, the City of Sydney has a 'vertical communities' program, designed to strengthen the social connections of people living in apartments. The move comes after a survey of residents revealed less than half were satisfied with feeling part of the community, with fifty-one per cent reporting they were neutral, unsatisfied or very unsatisfied. Little more than half thought they could get help from neighbours if needed.

Already, three-quarters of the city's population live in high-density apartments. This is expected to grow to ninety per cent – with forty per cent living alone. Across the country, however, research shows the biggest growth in solo households is actually across the middle and outer ring areas. With this in mind, it's important that architects, planners, developers and governments cater to everyone living alone, rather than just a single demographic.

Reflection

David: In this final chapter, we explored the changing nature of Australian families, with a continued increase in blended and stepfamilies, as well as grandparent and single-parent families. We then broached the topic of work-life balance among Australian women and, later, Michelle highlighted the pleasure and pain of being a member of Gen Y. In the second half of the chapter, we turned our focus to multigenerational living and the rise of solo households – two trends that are set to transform Australian families (and society more broadly) even further.

When reflecting on this chapter, consider:

- It is evident that, in many Australian families, grandparents will play an increasingly important role. To what extent will they feature in yours?
- How else might your family unit change in the future? How does this affect you?
- If you're a working mother, how do you approach work-life balance? If not, how do you support the working mothers in your immediate and broader family?
- If you're a member of Gen Y, what do you think of the comments made by Ita Buttrose? Is there any truth to them?
- If you're a baby boomer or a member of Gen X, do you recognise the pressures faced by the younger generations, namely Gen Y?
- What are your thoughts on multigenerational living? Would you ever consider it? Why or why not?

- What is your attitude towards the ageing members of your family? Do you think you could evolve your attitude? Why or why not?
- Who is living alone in your immediate family? How does this affect them?

Tapping into Positive Psychology

*'What humans want is not just happiness.
They want justice; they want meaning.'*

– **Martin Seligman**

In the preface of this book, we spoke about the power of systems thinking. Now, before we leave you, we want to touch on another theory that holds relevance in the context of this book: positive psychology. Specifically, we want to highlight the potential of the PERMA model.

Learned optimism and PERMA

*'Life inflicts the same setbacks and tragedies
on the optimist as on the pessimist, but
the optimist weathers them better.'*

– **Martin Seligman**

David: When visiting London in the mid-2010s, I met up with some friends. One of my friends had transformed his life, leaving a corporate job and founding a business focused on making people think and feel differently. I was intrigued to learn how he made this transition; he explained that he suffered from anxiety and didn't want to continue living like that. He also wanted to apply some techniques alone and consistently to progress in the direction he would prefer his life to take. He mentioned PERMA – a model developed by American psychologist Martin Seligman.

Seligman is referred to by some as the father of positive psychology and has written many self-help books on the topic. His most recent book, *The Hope Circuit: A Psychologist's Journey from Helplessness to Optimism*, chronicles his life and work. The book is a professional and personal memoir, interweaving research and personal experiences over seventy years.

In 1968, Seligman discovered by accident that dogs in an experimental conditioning protocol did not respond to opportunities to escape from an unpleasant situation. From this, Seligman developed his theory of learned helplessness. This a state that occurs after an animal or human being has experienced an unpleasant situation repeatedly. They come to believe that they are unable to control or change the situation, so they do not try – even when opportunities for change arise.

This prompted Seligman to wonder what other mindsets and perspectives can be learned, and whether people could develop positive traits instead of developing feelings of helplessness. His research led him to create the model of *learned optimism*, which is a concept of positive psychology.

Positive psychology focuses on people's strengths instead of their weaknesses, with the intent of building a good life rather than repairing the bad. It teaches people how to shift their perspective to maximise the potential for happiness in many of their everyday behaviours. An article at PositivePsychology.com summarises some of the research on this:

1. People overestimate the impact of money on their happiness by quite a lot. It has some influence, but not as much as you might think. Focusing less on attaining wealth will likely make you happier.
2. Money spent on experiences rather than material possessions offers a bigger boost to happiness.
3. Gratitude contributes greatly to one's happiness in life. The more someone cultivates gratitude, the happier they're likely to be.
4. Oxytocin appears to generate greater levels of trust, empathy and morality in humans. Giving someone a hug, or showing other types of physical affection, can significantly boost your overall wellbeing.
5. Intentionally cultivating a positive mood to match your outward emotional display can result in a more genuine positive mood – not because you have to 'put on a happy face', but because of the effort you make.
6. Happiness is contagious. People with happy partners and friends are more likely to be happy in the future.
7. People who show acts of kindness towards others are not only more accepted by their peers, but experience a boost in wellbeing.
8. People who volunteer their time to a cause they believe in benefit from improved wellbeing and life satisfaction.
9. Money spent on other people results in greater happiness for the giver.

In his book *Flourish: A Visionary New Understanding of Happiness and Well-Being*, Seligman states:

'I used to think that the topic of positive psychology was happiness, that the gold standard for measuring happiness was life satisfaction, and that the goal of positive psychology was to increase life satisfaction. I now think that the topic of positive psychology is well-being, that the gold standard

for measuring well-being is flourishing, and that the goal of positive psychology is to increase flourishing.'

In this book, Seligman introduced his PERMA model. This is made up of five elements that enable flourishing – **P**ositive Emotions, **E**ngagement, **R**elationships, **M**eaning and **A**ccomplishment – and there are techniques to increase each of them. Here's a quick overview of each element, from a website called Positive Psychology Training:

- **Positive Emotions**: These are an essential part of our wellbeing. Happy people look back on the past with gladness, look into the future with hope, and they enjoy and cherish the present.

- **Engagement**: When we focus on doing the things we truly enjoy and care about, we begin to engage completely with the present moment and enter the state of being known as 'flow'.

- **Relationships**: Everyone needs someone. We enhance our wellbeing and share it with others by building strong relationships with the people around us – family, friends, co-workers, neighbours.

- **Meaning**: We are at our best when we dedicate time to something greater than ourselves. This might be a religious faith, community work, family, politics, a charity, a professional or creative goal, or something else.

- **Accomplishment**: Everyone needs to win sometimes. To achieve wellbeing and happiness, we must be able to look back on our lives with a sense of accomplishment; 'I did it, and I did it well.'

Here are some of the ways I recognise the PERMA model in my own life:

- **Meaning is more important than money now.** My wife and I have built a secure life for our family, we have a home and we can earn income to meet our needs. There's a range of things I could be doing professionally, but some of these lack meaning for me. I am now focused on building a business based on work that has meaning to me, and using my greatest strengths within it.

- **Being present.** This means checking in with myself daily and asking myself whether I'm looking forward to the day ahead. Am I excited? What activities allow me to be immersed within them, and am I building more meaning in my life? If there is something that I am doing that is not meeting this criteria, I will either timebox the activity or slowly reduce my commitment to it over time if I am unable to stop it immediately.

- **Giving regularly to others.** My volunteering work at a university always puts a spring in my step afterwards, as there is a genuine connection with this community. Additionally, I make myself available to speak with those within my professional network who make contact. Often, this is just to chat through something they are wrestling with. These conversations serve me as much as the person I am speaking with. My weekly blog is sent to many people who are former colleagues and professional friends. I have zero expectations of anything in return, although I am grateful for those who choose to read it regularly.

- **Evolving and improving.** My life is not without worry or anxiety. There are times when I have both, particularly when I am waiting on a client's response to a proposal. These 'negative emotions' keep my saw sharp, resulting in refining the work I am doing. Quite simply, every book purchase, successful proposal and completed engagement has meaning. My chosen personal activity offers serenity and challenges daily. My yoga practice will never be perfect and that is why I keep returning to it. Plus, it adds so much to how I feel, boosts my mood and improves the quality of my thinking.

- **Being my true self.** What motivates me, what does not, and why? Everything that I choose to do is linked to my authentic self, improving myself and expressing myself to others. There is a constant focus on my place in the world. Specifically, how I can serve others while achieving a sense of accomplishment by bringing honesty and authenticity to everything I do.

The PERMA model was not consciously applied to my life; intuition led to these activities and the subsequent outcomes. This model offers potential for men in particular, in relation to how they can bring more meaning to their lives beyond their identity through their current job title.

Learning to flourish

'Changing the destructive things you say to yourself when you experience the setbacks that life deals all of us is the central skill of optimism.'

– Martin Seligman

Michelle: It's my sincere hope that you found value in this book, whether or not you agree with the views expressed by David and myself. In fact, I hope you don't agree with everything we've said. Ultimately, we want you to form your own opinions. Perhaps your opinions on certain topics have changed. Perhaps not.

Either way, we hope you'll step away from this book with a renewed sense of empowerment about your place in the world, and how you might bring more meaning not only to your own life but to the lives of others, too, by redefining what it means to be 'better'.

I had never heard of systems thinking or the PERMA model before I met David. These concepts have given me a much-needed reference point for my own thoughts, and for that I'm grateful. As David has already done, here are some of the ways I recognise the PERMA model in my life:

- **A new level of gratitude and positivity.** In 2020, it was easy to be buried by negativity. I have no doubt that every human on the planet felt it at some point. And while I had my fair share of dark moments that year, I also developed a deeper sense of gratitude for everything I have, and savoured all positive feelings in a way I had never done before.

- **Embracing the process, rather than focusing on the result.** As David and I were nearing the end of our writing journey, he asked me how this book would help my career. Truthfully, I'm not sure. For me, this book was always a passion project. To create something of meaning and offer it to the universe, simply because I could.

- **Living in the moment.** It wasn't until I experienced trauma that I was truly forced to live in the moment, with no real plan beyond the day ahead of me. When I say 'live in the moment', I don't mean less screen time or anything like that. I mean being confronted with something terrifying (in my case, it was my husband's stroke), and having no choice but to navigate it one day at a time. It was, and is, incredibly humbling. And while I didn't choose that experience, it has unquestionably strengthened my relationships with my husband, my family and myself.

- **'Getting ahead' means something different now.** As I highlighted earlier in the book, I was, for a time, obsessed with the idea of 'getting ahead'. It sounds clichéd, but it wasn't until I moved to a developing country (Thailand) that I realised how incredibly blessed I already am – and found meaning in so many things outside of money and material possessions. In fact, both of these things were in short supply for a while! And I believe I'm a better human for it.

- **Celebrating the end of every chapter.** Not every chapter of your life will be a happy one. Sometimes, the only cause for celebration is reaching the *end* of a chapter! But that in itself is an accomplishment. Not everything you experience has to be done 'well' or even shared publicly. Sometimes, simply surviving something is the biggest feat of all.

I encourage everyone, but especially women of my generation, to truly think about the PERMA model as it applies to them. Can you address each of the five elements in a positive way? Is there room for improvement anywhere, or perhaps a complete overhaul needed in one or more areas?

Whatever the case may be, having the courage to look inward and make the necessary changes will have flow-on effects that stem to your family, your community, your workplace, your country and beyond. Don't put off this important work – and never underestimate its impact.

Writing a Book with Someone You've Just Met

Not many first meetings end with a decision to write a book together. But that's exactly what happened when we met at the Subiaco Hotel in Perth on a warm evening in late February 2020. Neither of us knew just how momentous – or how fruitful – that meeting would turn out to be. Here, we both share our thoughts on the experience...and what it's like to write a book with someone you barely know.

David: It was an early summer evening on the 24th of February, a Monday, when I first met Michelle in person. I had only arrived in Perth that morning; my day started at about 2am and I was tired. I spent the day working with a client's finance leadership team, aligning them for a full-day workshop on Tuesday. Though something told me I needed to meet Michelle, it was not until late in the afternoon that I confirmed with her that we would meet.

We agreed to meet at the Subiaco Hotel, which was once a big, beautiful, traditional hotel that has now been renovated with a modern twist. I am not sure how these buildings will date. As always, I was slightly late, always trying to accommodate everyone with my time. Michelle waited patiently and when I walked in, I could see that her phone had kept her company. I thought this would be no more than a thirty-minute conversation.

I had recently published my first book and had told Michelle I was now thinking of writing a second book. My first book had a black cover, and I wanted the second book to have a white cover. This book would be completely different to my first. The first was about sharing my professional experiences and using this as a catalyst to build my business. This book is a letter to my children and grandchildren, and for anyone who thinks we could be doing a little better, as individuals and as a community, at sharing this planet.

As a former executive who spent years working sixty-plus hours a week, and regularly travelling away from home, I thought I could share some perspectives. These perspectives needed data; I needed a research person to help and I asked Michelle if she knew of anyone. Michelle kept asking about the book. Initially, I was not sure if she liked the idea. (I later learned that Michelle used to be a journalist. I was being interviewed, and the bonus for me was that these questions helped me refine my thinking.)

Those who have worked with me know I seek genuine feedback – the straighter the feedback, the better. So, I asked Michelle outright: Do you think the idea for this book is any good? I was waiting for a 'no'. It wasn't a 'no', but Michelle did offer some wisdom:

> *'I like the idea, but you're a white guy who is close to fifty and you probably don't know what it is like for the generation following yours. Also, I think the book could benefit from a woman's perspective.'*

I liked how forthright Michelle was, and so we decided that she and I would write the book together.

Our meeting suddenly turned into an informal workshop for the new book. All our ideas were captured by Michelle, who feverishly wrote everything down in a notebook. Many of the topics in this book were first discussed at that impromptu meeting. We huddled over the table for two and a half hours.

Michelle: As a Perth-based editor who works predominantly with clients on the east coast, it's not often that I get to meet my clients in person. So, when there's an opportunity to do so, I always say yes – and actually look forward to putting on a 'real' outfit and heading out into the world!

David and I had already spoken on the phone once or twice. I knew he'd spent part of his childhood in Perth, so we bonded on that basis. I knew he was very protective of his first book, having completed a small yet important post-publish editing job for him. I also knew he wanted me to edit his second book, but I didn't know what it was about.

David is very confident, yet also very calm. He practically glided into the Subiaco Hotel, set down his things and launched straight into the subject matter for his new book. As soon as he started talking about it, I knew I had to be involved. Not just as an editor, but as a contributor. The more he talked about it, the more I wanted to be a part of it. I had to stop myself from interrupting him every five seconds as new thoughts and ideas filled my head.

I had always thought about writing a book. But at thirty-three, I thought that perhaps I was still a little young and inexperienced. Who would want to hear what *I* had to say? But a little voice inside my head kept saying, 'This is it – this is your chance. You need to jump on this.' And so I did. When the moment was right, I said something along the lines of:

> *'Let me be really honest. You're a middle-aged, white guy. With all due respect, no matter how awesome your book is,*

*it will most likely appeal to other middle-aged, white guys...
and that's it. If we were co-editors, it would create more of a
dialogue in the book – one that's more balanced, since you're
male and I'm female. What do you think?'*

It was pretty ballsy – bordering on cheeky, really – but David liked
the idea. And so my next question was:

'Can I have a by-line?'

This was the moment of truth – everything hinged on David's
answer.

'Sure,' he said.

(David later admitted that he didn't actually know what a by-line
is! Luckily, he was still on board after I'd explained it to him.)

We'd also established that David was a proud member of Gen X
while I was unapologetically Gen Y. We thought our different
genders, ages and skills would create a strong point of difference
– and lead to some pretty interesting discussions. (And we were
right!)

At the meeting, David kept saying that he wanted this to be 'the
white book'. I didn't know what he meant by that, so I just nodded
and smiled. Only later, when I googled his first book (which I had
worked on as PDF, with no clue what the cover looked like), did
I realise that book was black – which is why he wanted his second
book to be white. It was a bit like the by-line thing – sometimes,
you have to fake it till you make it.

Writing a book with a new colleague is a bit like going on holiday
with a new partner. You see qualities in that other person, and so
you hope it will be a success, but you really just have to take a leap
of faith and figure it out as you go. Personally, I'm very glad I took
the plunge. David, thanks for jumping in the deep end with me.

References

Epigraph

Jobs, S. (1995). Interview with the Santa Clara Valley Historical Association. In Popova, M. (2011). 'The Secret of Life from Steve Jobs in 46 Seconds'. Brain Pickings, https://www.brainpickings.org/2011/12/02/steve-jobs-1995-life-failure/

Preface

Senge, P. (2016). 'Systems Thinking in a Digital World'. Dalai Lama Center for Peace and Education, https://www.youtube.com/watch?v=Zs3ML5ZJ_QY

Davidson, S., Morgan, M. (2018). 'Systems Change Framework', developed in partnership by The Australian Prevention Partnership Centre and the Tasmanian Department of Health. Sax Institute, https://preventioncentre.org.au/wp-content/uploads/2015/01/Systems-Change-Overview-w-Practices.pdf

Part 1: Country

Chapter 1

Bieber, F. (2018). 'Is Nationalism on the Rise? Assessing Global Trends'. Taylor & Francis Online, https://www.tandfonline.com/doi/full/10.1080/17449057.2018.1532633

Bloomberg. (2016). 'EU Referendum: Final Results'. *Bloomberg,* https://www.bloomberg.com/graphics/2016-brexit-referendum/

Cadwallar, C. and Graham-Harrison, E. (2018). 'Revealed: 50 million Facebook profiles harvested for Cambridge Analytica in major data breach'. *The Guardian,* https://www.theguardian.com/news/2018/mar/17/cambridge-analytica-facebook-influence-us-election

Ellyatt, H. (2020). "'It's not going to be the end of us': London's remain voters confront Brexit reality'. CNBC, https://www.cnbc.com/2020/01/30/londons-remain-voters-confront-brexit-reality.html

Enayati, A. (2012). 'The power of perceptions: Imagining the reality you want'. CNN, https://edition.cnn.com/2012/04/11/health/enayati-power-perceptions-imagination/index.html

Kimmel, M. (2017). *Angry White Men: American Masculinity at the End of an Era* (2nd ed). Bold Type Books

Krohn, C. (1999). 'Online Political Advertising: Our Salesman Reports'. *Slate*, https://slate.com/news-and-politics/1999/09/online-political-advertising-our-salesman-reports.html

Lau, T. (2020). 'The Honest Ads Act Explained'. The Brennan Center for Justice, https://www.brennancenter.org/our-work/research-reports/honest-ads-act-explained

Lee, C. E. and Kent, J. L. (2017). 'Facebook Says Russian-Backed Election Content Reached 126 Million Americans'. NBC News, https://www.nbcnews.com/news/us-news/russian-backed-election-content-reached-126-million-americans-facebook-says-n815791

Lotto, B. (2009). 'Optical illusions show how we see'. TED Talks, https://www.ted.com/talks/beau_lotto_optical_illusions_show_how_we_see

Siddiqui, S. (2019). 'Half of Americans see fake news as bigger threat than terrorism, study finds'. *The Guardian*, https://www.theguardian.com/us-news/2019/jun/06/fake-news-how-misinformation-became-the-new-front-in-us-political-warfare

Smith, H. (2020). 'Veteran journalist explains how 2020 campaign spending went through the roof'. *The Progressive Pulse*, http://pulse.ncpolicywatch.org/2020/11/30/2020-campaign-spending-goes-through-the-roof/#sthash.5zRZHMXS.dpbs

The Economist. (2020). 'Britons are increasingly avoiding the news'. *The Economist,* https://www.economist.com/britain/2020/08/20/britons-are-increasingly-avoiding-the-news

Weir, K. (2017). 'Why we believe alternative facts'. American Psychological Association, https://www.apa.org/monitor/2017/05/alternative-facts

Wong, J. C. (2018). 'It might work too well': the dark art of political advertising online'. *The Guardian,* https://www.theguardian.com/technology/2018/mar/19/facebook-political-ads-social-media-history-online-democracy

Chapter 2

Ashton, R. (2018). 'Short-term thinking is creating long-term problems'. *The Sydney Morning Herald,* https://www.smh.com.au/national/short-term-thinking-is-creating-long-term-problems-20181107-p50egn.html

Australian Government. (2020). 'Australian Government funding to the states, Budget Paper No.3'. Australian Government, https://budget.gov.au/2019-20/content/bp3/download/bp3_01_states.pdf

Beyond Federation. (2014). 'State Government Study'. Galaxy Research, http://members.webone.com.au/~markld/PubPol/GSR/Polls/Galaxy%20State%20Government%20Study%20May%202014.pdf

Burck, J., Hagen, U., Höhne, N., Nascimento, L., Bals, C. (2020). 'Climate Change Performance Index: Results 2020'. Germanwatch, NewClimate Institute, Climate Action Network International, https://newclimate.org/wp-content/uploads/2019/12/CCPI-2020-Results_Web_Version.pdf

Chesters, J., Cook, J., Cuervo, H., and Wyn, J. (2018). 'Examining the most important issues in Australia: similarities and differences across two generations'. Melbourne Graduate School of Education, The University of Melbourne,

https://education.unimelb.edu.au/__data/assets/pdf_
file/0011/2887895/Most-important-issues-report-final-
Sept-2018.pdf

Clench, S. and Khalil, S. (2019). 'Australia's most trusted politician
is New Zealand Prime Minister Jacinda Ardern'. News.com.
au, https://www.news.com.au/national/federal-election/
australias-most-trusted-politician-is-new-zealand-prime-
minister-jacinda-ardern/news-story/1e8dde03e31c0f9ffce2f83
cae64c476

CSIRO. (2019). 'Australian National Outlook 2019'. CSIRO,
https://www.csiro.au/en/Showcase/ANO

Harris, B. (2017). 'Heed Hawke's call – Australia federalism is
an idea whose time has ended'. *The Conversation*, https://
theconversation.com/heed-hawkes-call-australian-federalism-
is-an-idea-whose-time-has-ended-71001

Hewson, J. (2020). 'Enough of the short-term politics – we need
a government that leads'. *The Age*, https://www.theage.com.
au/politics/federal/enough-of-the-short-term-politics-we-
need-a-government-that-leads-20201118-p56fqb.html

Kehoe, J. (2019). 'Why Australia is falling behind on productivity.
The Australian Financial Review, https://www.afr.com/
technology/wages-hurt-by-low-tech-adoption-and-less-job-
switching-20190619-p51zbc

Murphy, K. (2019). 'Malcolm Turnbull says Liberals' struggles
with climate denial are hurting Australia'. *The Guardian*,
https://www.theguardian.com/australia-news/2019/nov/23/
malcolm-turnbull-says-liberals-struggles-with-climate-denial-
are-hurting-australia

Remeikis, A. (2016). 'Bob Hawke says abolish state governments
and think big to fix the nation'. *The Sydney Morning Herald*,
https://www.smh.com.au/politics/federal/bob-hawke-says-
abolish-state-governments-and-think-big-to-fix-the-nation-
20161228-gtiwgv.html

Roser, M. (2013). 'Economic Growth'. Our World in Data, https://ourworldindata.org/economic-growth

Smith, A. (2020). 'New Zealand's Jacinda Ardern wins big after world-leading Covid-19 response'. NBC News, https://www.nbcnews.com/news/world/new-zealand-s-jacinda-ardern-wins-big-after-world-leading-n1243972

Taylor, J. (2019). 'Q&A: short-term 'tribal' politics is failing on climate action, John Hewson says'. *The Guardian*, https://www.theguardian.com/australia-news/2019/oct/22/qa-short-term-tribal-politics-is-failing-on-climate-action-john-hewson-says

The University of Melbourne. 'Life Patterns'. Research Program, The University of Melbourne, https://education.unimelb.edu.au/yrc/research/life-patterns

Weill, P., Dery, K., and Woerner, S. (2020). 'Australian firms need to become future ready'. MIT Center for Information Systems Research, https://cisr.mit.edu/publication/2020_0601a_AUSPathways_WeillDeryWoerner

Part 2: Workplace

Chapter 3

Bernard, Z. (2018). 'The idea that most successful startup founders are in their twenties is a myth – the average entrepreneur is much older'. *Business Insider Australia*, https://www.businessinsider.com.au/young-startup-founder-myth-average-age-of-entrepreneurs-42-mit-study-2018-4?r=US&IR–T

Bowenbank, S. (2020). 'Princess Sofia of Sweden Is Volunteering at a Local Hospital During the Coronavirus Pandemic'. *Cosmopolitan*, https://www.cosmopolitan.com/entertainment/celebs/a32223814/princess-sofia-of-sweden-volunteering-coronavirus-pandemic/

Eadicicco, L. (2019). 'Microsoft experimented with a 4-day workweek, and productivity jumped by 40%'. *Business Insider*

Australia, https://www.businessinsider.com.au/microsoft-4-day-work-week-boosts-productivity-2019-11?r=US&IR=T

Edmonson, A. (2014). 'Building a psychologically safe workplace'. TEDx Talks, https://www.youtube.com/watch?v=LhoLuui9gX8&feature=youtu.be

Eurostat. (2018). 'How many hours do Europeans work per week?' European Commission, Eurostat, https://ec.europa.eu/eurostat/web/products-eurostat-news/-/DDN-20180125-1

Fox, M. (2019) 'Forget the 5-day work week – just 4 days results in 'a healthier, more loyal, more engaged staff''. CNBC, https://www.cnbc.com/2019/04/23/a-4-day-work-week-results-in-more-loyal-more-engaged-staff.html

GEM Consortium. (2019). 'Global Entrepreneurship Monitor: 2018/2019 Report'. GEM, https://www.gemconsortium.org/report/gem-2018-2019-global-report

Glassdoor. (2017). 'Glassdoor survey finds Americans forfeit half of their earned vacation/paid time off'. Glassdoor, https://www.glassdoor.com/about-us/glassdoor-survey-finds-americans-forfeit-earned-vacationpaid-time/

Google re:Work. 'Guide: Understand team effectiveness'. Google re:Work, https://rework.withgoogle.com/print/guides/5721312655835136/

Hanrahan, M. (2017). 'France 'Right to Disconnect' Law: Do We Need Rules To Reclaim Personal Time?' NBC News, https://www.nbcnews.com/news/world/france-right-disconnect-law-do-we-need-rules-reclaim-personal-n704366

Knight, N. (2016). 'The 17th century warship that sank, was recovered & is now in a museum for all to see...' *The Vintage News*, https://www.thevintagenews.com/2016/08/07/the-17th-century-warship-that-sank-was-recovered-is-now-in-a-museum-for-all-to-see-2/

Lane, E. (2017). 'The young Japanese working themselves to death'. BBC News, https://www.bbc.com/news/business-39981997

Lebowitz, S. (2018). ''Entrepreneurship porn' lures young people with a pretty picture of startup life, but it glosses over the most dangerous parts'. *Business Insider Australia*, https://www.businessinsider.com.au/starting-business-entrepreneurship-hard-7-2018-7

Maack, M. M. (2017). 'Scandinavian work culture is better than yours – here's why'. The Next Web, https://thenextweb.com/business/2017/02/20/scandinavian-work-culture-is-better-than-yours/

Mendoza, N. F. (2020). 'COVID-19 has exacerbated a 75% job burnout rate, study says'. Tech Republic, https://www.techrepublic.com/article/covid-19-has-exacerbated-a-75-job-burnout-rate-study-says/

MIT Sloan Experts Series. (2020). ''Human-centred AI': How can the technology industry fight bias in machines and people?' Webcast, MIT Sloan, https://mitsloan.mit.edu/press

Norman, R. T. (2020). 'What is Janteloven?' Scandinavia Standard, https://www.scandinaviastandard.com/what-is-janteloven-the-law-of-jante/

Northcote Parkinson, C. (1955). 'Parkinson's Law'. *The Economist*, https://www.economist.com/news/1955/11/19/parkinsons-law

Peters, A. (2019) 'This New Zealand company proves how 4-day workweeks are great for business'. Fast Company, https://www.fastcompany.com/90325704/this-new-zealand-company-proves-how-4-day-work-weeks-are-great-for-business

Sandemose, A. (1936). *A Fugitive Crosses His Tracks*. Alfred A. Knopf strivetoengage. (2017). 'You shall not think you are anybody special – reflections on "Janteloven"'. strivetoengage blog, https://strivetoengage.wordpress.com/2017/03/11/you-shall-not-think-you-are-anybody-special-reflections-on-janteloven/

United Nations. (2017). 'New globalization report: Three mega-trends expected to impact our future'. United Nations, Department of Economic and Social Affairs, https://www.un.org/development/desa/en/news/intergovernmental-coordination/new-globalization-report.html

Wasserman, N. (2013). *The Founder's Dilemmas: Anticipating and Avoiding the Pitfalls That Can Sink a Startup.* Princeton University Press

Xuequiao, W. and Hancock, T. (2019). 'Overdoing it: the cost of China's long-hours culture'. *Financial Times,* https://www.ft.com/content/d5f01f68-9cbc-11e8-88de-49c908b1f264

Chapter 4

Australian Government. (2018). 'Industry Insights: 3/2018 Future productivity'. Australian Government, Department of Industry, Innovation and Science, https://publications.industry.gov.au/publications/industryinsightsjune2018/future-productivity.html

Australian Men's Shed Association. 'About Men's Sheds'. Webpage, AMSA, https://mensshed.org/what-is-a-mens-shed/

BBC Worklife. (2020). 'Coronavirus: How the world of work may change forever'. BBC, https://www.bbc.com/worklife/article/20201023-coronavirus-how-will-the-pandemic-change-the-way-we-work

Buffer & AngelList. (2020). 'The 2020 State of Remote Work'. Buffer, https://lp.buffer.com/state-of-remote-work-2020

Correll, S. J. and Simard, C. (2016). 'Research: Vague Feedback Is Holding Women Back'. *Harvard Business Review*, https://hbr.

org/2016/04/research-vague-feedback-is-holding-women-back

Davim, C., Dempster, A. (2020). 'COVID-19: Protecting the mental health of remote workforces'. KPMG, https://home.kpmg/au/en/home/insights/2020/04/coronavirus-covid-19-protecting-mental-health-of-remote-workforce.html

Ferrante, M. B. (2018). 'The Pressure Is Real For Working Mothers'. *Forbes*, https://www.forbes.com/sites/marybethferrante/2018/08/27/the-pressure-is-real-for-working-mothers

Gartner. (2019). 'Gartner Survey Shows CIOs in Australia and New Zealand Are Making Slow Digital Business Progress'. PRWire, https://prwire.com.au/pr/83557/gartner-survey-shows-cios-in-australia-and-new-zealand-are-making-slow-digital-business-progress

Khazan, O. (2017). 'Why Do Women Bully Each Other at Work?' *The Atlantic*, https://www.theatlantic.com/magazine/archive/2017/09/the-queen-bee-in-the-corner-office/534213/

Macmillan, A. (2017). 'Women Are Judged Whether They Take Maternity Leave Or Not'. *Time*, https://time.com/4804027/maternity-leave-in-the-us/

Moreno, J. (2019). 'Google Follows A Growing Workplace Trend: Hiring More Contractors Than Employees'. *Forbes,* https://www.forbes.com/sites/johanmoreno/2019/05/31/google-follows-a-growing-workplace-trend-hiring-more-contractors-than-employees/?sh=d8fdc4b447fe

Morgenroth, T., Heilman, M. E. (2017). 'Should I stay or should I go? Implications of maternity leave choice for perceptions of working mothers'. Journal of Experimental Social Psychology, Volume 72, Pages 53-56, https://www.sciencedirect.com/science/article/pii/S0022103116307788

Robert Half. (2019). 'The rise of the gig economy: One third of global workforce expected to be contractors by 2023'.

Robert Half, https://www.roberthalf.com.au/press/rise-gig-economy-one-third-global-workforce-expected-be-contractors-2023

SBS News. (2019). 'Australians flock to gig economy for work'. SBS News, https://www.sbs.com.au/news/australians-flock-to-gig-economy-for-work

Schumacher, H. (2019). 'Why more men than women die by suicide'. BBC Future, https://www.bbc.com/future/article/20190313-why-more-men-kill-themselves-than-women

Shiao, V. (2016). 'Why we don't like women bosses (and why it matters)'. *The Business Times*, https://www.businesstimes.com.sg/opinion/why-we-dont-like-women-bosses-and-why-it-matters

Simon-Davies, J. (2019). 'International Men's Health Week'. Parliament of Australia, https://www.aph.gov.au/About_Parliament/Parliamentary_Departments/Parliamentary_Library/FlagPost/2019/June/Mens_health

State Government of Victoria. (2019). 'Revealing The True Size of Australia's Gig Workforce'. Department of Premier and Cabinet, State Government of Victoria, https://www.premier.vic.gov.au/revealing-true-size-australias-gig-workforce

Venker, S. (2019). 'Work is at the core of a man's identity'. *Washington Examiner,* https://www.washingtonexaminer.com/opinion/work-is-at-the-core-of-a-mans-identity

Ye, R., Ma, L. (2019). 'Australian city workers' average commute has blown out to 66 minutes a day. How does yours compare?' SBS News, https://www.sbs.com.au/news/australian-city-workers-average-commute-has-blown-out-to-66-minutes-a-day-how-does-yours-compare

Part 3: Community

Chapter 5

Befrienders Worldwide. 'Suicide Statistics'. Webpage, Befrienders Worldwide, https://www.befrienders.org/suicide-statistics

Beyond Blue. 'Depression in Men'. Webpage, Beyond Blue, https://www.beyondblue.org.au/who-does-it-affect/men/depression-in-men

Bryn Mawr Hospital. (2018). 'Recognizing male midlife depression and anger'. Main Line Health, https://www.mainlinehealth.org/blog/2018/07/05/depression-in-men

Carey, B. and Gebeloff, R. (2018). 'Many People Taking Antidepressants Discover They Cannot Quit'. *The New York Times*, https://www.nytimes.com/2018/04/07/health/antidepressants-withdrawal-prozac-cymbalta.html

Cartwright, C., Gibson, K., Read, J., Cowan, O., and Dehar, T. (2016). 'Long-term antidepressant use: patient perspectives of benefits and adverse effects'. Patient Preference and Adherence, https://www.ncbi.nlm.nih.gov/pmc/articles/PMC4970636/

Dyer, T. 'Prescription Drug Abuse'. DrugRehab.com, https://www.drugrehab.com/addiction/prescription-drugs/

Gottfried, S. (2019). 'Niksen Is the Dutch Lifestyle Concept of Doing Nothing – And You're About to See It Everywhere'. *Time*, https://time.com/5622094/what-is-niksen/

Helweg-Larsen, M. (2018)'Americans don't need more money to be happier – they need to be like Denmark'. Quartz, https://qz.com/1235050/hygge-is-the-reason-denmark-is-consistently-happier-than-america/

Ingber, S. (2018). 'Former Republican House Speaker Is Advising A Marijuana Corporation'. NPR, https://www.npr.org/sections/thetwo-way/2018/04/11/601655200/former-republican-house-speaker-is-advising-a-marijuana-corporation

Kovary, G. (2016). 'The "Semi-Retired" Gen Xer'. n-gen, https://www.ngenperformance.com/blog/leadership-2/the-semi-retired-gen-xer

Margolies, L. (2016). 'Midlife Crises Affecting Men and Families'. Psych Central, https://psychcentral.com/lib/midlife-crises-affecting-men-and-families#1

Murse, T. (2020). 'States Where Smoking Recreational Marijuana Is Legal'. Thought Co., https://www.thoughtco.com/states-that-legalized-marijuana-3368391

National Institute on Drug Abuse. (2021). 'Overdose Death Rates'. NIH, National Institute on Drug Abuse, https://www.drugabuse.gov/drug-topics/trends-statistics/overdose-death-rates

NHS Digital. (2016). 'Antidepressants show greatest increase in number of prescription items dispensed'. NHS Digital. https://webarchive.nationalarchives.gov.uk/20180328132302/http://content.digital.nhs.uk/article/7159/Antidepressants-show-greatest-increase-in-number-of-prescription-items-dispensed

Nicodemus, R. 'Packing Party: Unpack a Simpler Life'. The Minimalists, https://www.theminimalists.com/packing/

Plumbing & Mechanical. (2015). 'Hansgrohe study: The brightest ideas begin in the shower'. Plumbing & Mechanical, https://www.pmmag.com/articles/96968-hansgrohe-study-the-brightest-ideas-begin-in-the-shower

Read, J., Cartwright, C., Gibson, K. (2018). 'How many of 1829 antidepressant users report withdrawal effects or addiction?' Int J Ment Health Nurs., https://pubmed.ncbi.nlm.nih.gov/29873165/

Sarris, J., Sinclair, J., Karamacoska, D., Davidson, M. and Firth, J. (2020). 'Medicinal cannabis for psychiatric disorders: a clinically-focused systematic review'. BMC Psychiatry 20, 24, https://bmcpsychiatry.biomedcentral.com/articles/10.1186/s12888-019-2409-8

Shapiro, L. (2018). 'Antidepressant Withdrawal: Are the Benefits Worth the Risk of Dependence?' US Recall News, https://www.usrecallnews.com/antidepressant-withdrawal-are-the-benefits-worth-the-risk-of-dependence/

The Withdrawal Project. 'Are you thinking about coming off psychiatric drugs?' Webpage, Inner Compass Initiative, https://withdrawal.theinnercompass.org/

Tiny House Citizens. (2020). '10 Benefits of Living in a Tiny House'. Tiny House Citizens, https://tinyhousecitizens.com/10-benefits-living-tiny-house/

World Health Organisation. 'Mental Health'. Webpage, WHO, https://www.who.int/mental_health/prevention/suicide/background/en/

Yoga Journal Editors. (2017). '10 Men Share How They Got Hooked On Yoga'. Yoga Journal, https://www.yogajournal.com/poses/10-men-hooked-on-yoga/

Chapter 6

Alcohol and Drug Foundation. (2019). 'Role modelling alcohol consumption'. ADF, https://adf.org.au/insights/role-modelling-alcohol-consumption/

American Psychological Association. (2018). 'APA Guidelines for Psychological Practice with Boys and Men'. American Psychological Association, https://www.apa.org/about/policy/boys-men-practice-guidelines.pdf

Australian Psychological Society and the University of Swinburne. (2018). 'Australian Loneliness Report'. Psychology Week 2018, https://psychweek.org.au/wp/wp-content/uploads/2018/11/Psychology-Week-2018-Australian-Loneliness-Report-1.pdf

Flood, M. (2018). 'Australian study reveals the dangers of 'toxic masculinity' to men and those around them'. The Conversation, https://theconversation.com/australian-study-reveals-the-dangers-of-toxic-masculinity-to-men-and-those-around-them-104694

Foundation for Alcohol Research and Education. (2019). '2019 Annual Alcohol Poll: Attitudes and Behaviours'. FARE, https://fare.org.au/wp-content/uploads/FARE-Annual-Alcohol-Poll-2019-FINAL.pdf

Gerrans, M. (2018). 'Drinking Culture in Australia'. Insider Guides, https://insiderguides.com.au/alcohol-in-australia/

Granovetter, M. (1973). 'The Strength of Weak Ties'. American Journal of Sociology 78, 1360-80

Greer, G. (2006). 'That sort of self-delusion is what it takes to be a real Aussie larrikin'. *The Guardian,* https://www.theguardian.com/world/2006/sep/05/australia

Hofstede, G. (2001). *Culture's consequences: Comparing values, behaviors, institutions, and organizations across nations.* Thousand Oaks, CA: Sage Publications.

Hofstede, G., Hofstede G. J., and Minkov, M. (2010). *Cultures and organizations: Software of the mind.* Revised and Expanded 3rd Edition. New York: McGraw-Hill.

Hofstede Insights. 'Country Comparison'. Webpage. Hofstede Insights. https://www.hofstede-insights.com/country-comparison/australia,the-netherlands,sweden/

Huntley, R. (2019) 'Volunteering benefits our community and society, but rates are declining'. ABC Everyday, https://www.abc.net.au/everyday/benefits-of-volunteering-to-community-and-society/11075998

Jennings-Edquist, G. (2018). 'Feeling isolated? You're not alone. Here's why 1 in 4 of us is lonely'. ABC Everyday, https://www.abc.net.au/everyday/social-isolation-why-are-we-so-lonely/10493414

Karp, P. (2020). 'Australia's volunteer firefighting force declined 10% in past decade'. *The Guardian,* https://www.theguardian.

com/australia-news/2020/jan/29/australias-volunteer-firefighting-force-declined-10-in-past-decade

Kitchener, C. (2020). 'I had to choose being a mother': With no child care or summer camps, women are being edged out of the workforce.' *The Lily, The Washington Post,* https://www.thelily.com/i-had-to-choose-being-a-mother-with-no-child-care-or-summer-camps-women-are-being-edged-out-of-the-workforce/

Laslett, A., Room, R., Waleewong, O., Stanesby, O. and Callinan, S. (2019). 'Harm to Others by Drinking: Patterns in Nine Societies'. WHO, https://apps.who.int/iris/bitstream/handle/10665/329393/9789241515368-eng.pdf?sequence=1&isAllowed=y

Leslie, I. (2020). 'Why your 'weak-tie' friendships may mean more than you think'. BBC Worklife, https://www.bbc.com/worklife/article/20200701-why-your-weak-tie-friendships-may-mean-more-than-you-think

Promundo and the University of Pittsburgh. 'Manhood 2.0'. Gender-transformative initiative, Promundo, https://promundoglobal.org/programs/manhood-2-0/

Southern Cross University. (2016). 'Young men can learn to curb their anger and aggressive behaviour: new study finds'. Southern Cross University, https://www.scu.edu.au/engage/news/latest-news/2014/young-men-can-learn-to-curb-their-anger-and-aggressive-behaviour-new-study-finds.php

Stewart, B., Nicholson, M., Smith. A., Westerbeek, H. (2004). *Australian Sport – Better by Design?: The Evolution of Australian Sport Policy* (1st ed). Routledge

The Men's Project & Flood, M. (2018). 'The Man Box: A study on being a young man in Australia'. Jesuit Social Services: Melbourne, https://jss.org.au/wp-content/uploads/2018/10/The-Man-Box-A-study-on-being-a-young-man-in-Australia.pdf

The University of Queensland Business School. (2016). 'Revealed: how alcohol is at the heart of local sport'. The University of Queensland Business School, https://business.uq.edu.au/momentum/revealed-how-alcohol-heart-local-sport

Vaynerchuk, G. (2019). 'How to Stop Caring What Others Think'. garyvaynerchuk.com, https://www.garyvaynerchuk.com/how-to-stop-caring-what-others-think/

Volunteering Australia. (2015). 'Are time poor Australians abandoning volunteering?' Volunteering Australia, https://www.volunteeringaustralia.org/wp-content/uploads/Media-Release-ABS-General-Social-Survey.pdf

Watson, S. (2013). 'Volunteering may be good for body and mind'. Harvard Health Publishing, https://www.health.harvard.edu/blog/volunteering-may-be-good-for-body-and-mind-201306266428

Part 4: Family

Chapter 7

ABC News. (2020). 'Federal Treasurer forecasts difficult economic recovery after coronavirus recession amid slump in population growth, low interest rates'. ABC News, https://www.abc.net.au/news/2020-07-24/treasurer-josh-frydenberg-baby-boom-economy-recovery-coronavirus/12489678

Acosta, R. M. (2019). 'This popular parenting trend in the Netherlands reveals a key to raising the world's happiest kids'. CNBC, https://www.cnbc.com/2019/08/29/dutch-fathers-play-a-big-role-in-raising-the-happies-kids-in-the-world.html

Baxter, J. (2018). 'Fathers and Work: A statistical overview'. Australian Institute of Family Studies, https://aifs.gov.au/sites/default/files/publication-documents/4_fathers_and_work_1904.pdf

Boteck, A. (2017). Sons vs. Daughters: The Role of Gender in Caring for Aging Parents'. Aging Care, https://www.

agingcare.com/articles/daughters-care-more-for-parents-than-sons-171474.htm

Brooker, D. (2019). '3 Simple Insights Melinda Gates Shared At The Moment Of Lift Book Talk In London'. *Forbes*, https://www.forbes.com/sites/daniellebrooker/2019/07/28/3-simple-insights-melinda-gates-shared-at-the-moment-of-lift-book-talk-in-london/

Buchanan, A. and Rotkirch, A. (2018) 'Twenty-first century grandparents: global perspectives on changing roles and consequences'. Contemporary Social Science, 13:2, 131-144, Taylor & Francis Online, https://www.tandfonline.com/doi/full/10.1080/21582041.2018.1467034

Cain Miller, C. (2020). 'Nearly Half of Men Say They Do Most of the Homeschooling. 3 Percent of Women Agree.' *The New York Times*, https://www.nytimes.com/2020/05/06/upshot/pandemic-chores-homeschooling-gender.html

Calhoun, A. (2020). *Why We Can't Sleep: Women's New Midlife Crisis*. Grove Press UK.

Dorney, G. (2019). 'Dads want to take time off work for their kids, so why aren't they?' HRM Online, Australian HR Institute, https://www.hrmonline.com.au/parental-leave/dads-work-kids/

Dotti Sani, G., Treas, J. (2016). Journal of Marriage and Family 78 (August 2016): 1083–1096, https://onlinelibrary.wiley.com/doi/epdf/10.1111/jomf.12305

Feller, B. (2017). 'App Time for Nap Time: The Parennials Are Here'. *The New York Times,* https://www.nytimes.com/2017/11/04/style/millennial-parents-parennials.html.

Flaherty, C. (2018). 'Dancing Backwards in High Heels'. Inside Higher Ed, https://www.insidehighered.com/news/2018/01/10/study-finds-female-professors-experience-more-work-demands-and-special-favor

Gallagher, J. (2020). 'Fertility rate: 'Jaw-dropping' global crash in children being born'. BBC News, https://www.bbc.com/news/health-53409521

Hamlyn, C. (2018). 'Baby boomers move in with adults kids as multi-generational housing trend changes how we live'. ABC News, https://www.abc.net.au/news/2018-08-19/the-baby-boomers-moving-in-with-their-adult-kids/10126404

Harris, B. (2018). 'These are the happiest countries in the world'. World Economic Forum, https://www.weforum.org/agenda/2018/03/these-are-the-happiest-countries-in-the-world/

Haynes, T. (2018). 'Dopamine, Smartphones & You: A battle for your time'. SITNBoston, Harvard University, http://sitn.hms.harvard.edu/flash/2018/dopamine-smartphones-battle-time/

Home-Start. (2019). '#RealLifeParenting'. Blog, Home-Start, https://www.home-start.org.uk/blogs/reallifeparenting

Jeffries, S., Konnert, C. (2002). 'Regret and psychological well-being among voluntarily and involuntarily childless women and mothers'. Int J Aging Hum Dev. 2002;54(2):89-106. NIH, https://pubmed.ncbi.nlm.nih.gov/12054274/

Lebowitz, S. (2017). 'Prince Harry reportedly wants to be a 'modern dad' and to ask the queen for paternity leave. Here are 20 ways millennials are raising kids differently than any generation before them'. *Business Insider Australia*, https://www.businessinsider.com.au/differences-millennial-gen-x-baby-boomer-parents-2017-11?r=US&IR=T

Marte, J. (2015). 'Why parenting is even more daunting for millennials than it was for their parents – or their grandparents'. *The Washington Post*. https://www.washingtonpost.com/news/get-there/wp/2015/04/29/the-catch-22-many-millennial-parents-face/

McKenna, J. (2018). 'This is why Dutch teenagers are among the happiest in the world'. World Economic Forum, https://www.

weforum.org/agenda/2018/06/this-is-why-dutch-teenagers-are-among-the-happiest-in-the-world/

Naysmith, S. (2019). 'Picture perfect families on social media are driving real parents to despair, survey finds'. *The Herald*, https://www.heraldscotland.com/news/17955327.picture-perfect-families-social-media-driving-real-parents-despair-survey-finds/

Pew Research Center. (2015). 'Parenting in America: The American family today'. Pew Research Center https://www.pewsocialtrends.org/2015/12/17/1-the-american-family-today/

Pew Research Center. (2015). 'Parenting in America: Outlook, worries, aspirations are strongly linked to financial situation'. Pew Research Center, https://www.pewsocialtrends.org/2015/12/17/parenting-in-america/

Piskorz, J. (2018). 'Me and my quarter-life crisis: a millennial asks what went wrong'. *The Guardian*. https://www.theguardian.com/global/2018/dec/30/me-and-my-quarter-life-crisis-a-millennial-asks-what-went-wrong

Schmall, T. (2018). 'First comes baby, then comes baby's personalized domain name'. *New York Post*, https://nypost.com/2018/08/16/first-comes-baby-then-comes-babys-personalized-domain-name/

Schulte, B. (2019). 'A woman's greatest enemy? A lack of time to herself'. *The Guardian,* https://www.theguardian.com/commentisfree/2019/jul/21/woman-greatest-enemy-lack-of-time-themselves

Scott, K. (2019). 'More women are choosing not to have kids, and society can't cope'. ABC Everyday, https://www.abc.net.au/everyday/more-women-are-choosing-not-to-have-kids-and-society-cannot-cope/11160788

Smith, P. M., Cawley, C., Williams, A. Mustard, C. (2019). Male/Female Differences in the Impact of Caring for Elderly

Relatives on Labor Market Attachment and Hours of Work: 1997-2015'. The Journals of Gerontology: Series B, Volume 75, Issue 3, March 2020, Pages 694–704. Oxford Academic, Oxford University Press, https://academic.oup.com/psychsocgerontology/article/75/3/694/5423973

Time. (2015). 'How Millennial Parents Think Differently About Raising Kids'. *Time,* https://time.com/4070021/millennial-parents-raising-kids-poll/

Vollset, S. E., Goren, E., Yuan, C., Cao, J., Smith, A. E., Hsiao, T., et al. (2020). 'Fertility, mortality, migration, and population scenarios for 195 countries and territories from 2017to 2100: a forecasting analysis for the Global Burden of Disease Study'. *The Lancet,* https://www.thelancet.com/journals/lancet/article/PIIS0140-6736(20)30677-2/fulltext

Walsh, L. (2017). 'Perils of perfection: Social media is ramping up the pressure on young people to be perfect'. *The Advertiser,* News.com.au, https://www.news.com.au/lifestyle/parenting/perils-of-perfection-social-media-is-ramping-up-the-pressure-on-young-people-to-be-perfect/news-story/7cb9cac2cf26d4f0 0673f3a9fdf6380e#bottom-share

Weber-Raley, L. (2019). 'November 2019 National Report. Burning the Candle at Both Ends: Sandwich Generation Caregiving Across the US'. National Alliance for Caregiving and Caring Across Generations, https://caringacross.org/wp-content/uploads/2019/11/NAC_SandwichCaregiving_Report_digital112019.pdf

Chapter 8

Australian Bureau of Statistics. (2017). '2016 Census'. ABS. https://www.abs.gov.au/websitedbs/censushome.nsf/home/2016

Australian Bureau of Statistics. (2019). 'Household and Family Projections, Australia'. Australian Bureau of Statistics, https://

www.abs.gov.au/statistics/people/population/household-and-family-projections-australia/latest-release

Australian Institute of Health and Welfare. (2017). 'Australia's Welfare 2017'. Australia's welfare series no. 13. AUS 214. Canberra: AIHW, https://www.aihw.gov.au/getmedia/088848dc-906d-4a8b-aa09-79df0f943984/aihw-aus-214-aw17.pdf.aspx?inline=true

Australian Unity. 'Australian Unity Wellbeing Index'. The Australian Centre on Quality of Life, Deakin University, https://www.australianunity.com.au/media-centre/wellbeing

Bialik, K. and Fry, R. (2019). 'Millennial life: How young adulthood today compares with prior generations'. Pew Research Center, https://www.pewsocialtrends.org/essay/millennial-life-how-young-adulthood-today-compares-with-prior-generations/

Bowen, A. (2017). '5 things high-powered women need to know about work-life balance'. *Chicago Tribune.* https://www.chicagotribune.com/lifestyles/sc-fam-female-executives-work-life-balance-0718-story.html

Campbell, D. R., Hunt, J. Wissink, R. (2019). 'The Millennial Report'. The Real Estate Intelligence Network, http://cdn3.reincanada.com/Research/REIN_The_Millennial_Report_DIGITAL.pdf

CareSearch. (2018). 'Living Alone'. CareSearch, https://www.caresearch.com.au/caresearch/ClinicalPractice/SpecificPopulations/LivingAlone/tabid/1417/Default.aspx

Churchill, B. (2018). 'Forget the 'norm' the Australian family is changing'. Insight, SBS, https://www.sbs.com.au/news/insight/forget-the-norm-the-australian-family-is-changing

Connolly, J. (2019). 'Multi-generational living, space-sharing and other Millennial home-buying hacks'. Vancouver is Awesome, Glacier Media Group, https://www.vancourier.com/real-estate/multi-generational-living-space-sharing-and-other-millennial-home-buying-hacks-1.23867896

CVCheck. 'What work-life balance really looks like for women in 2020'. Check Point, CVCheck, https://checkpoint.cvcheck.com/what-work-life-balance-really-looks-like-for-women-in-2020/

Huntley, R. (2019). 'Young people living at home longer is often seen as a bad thing – but is it?' ABC Everyday, https://www.abc.net.au/everyday/young-people-living-at-home-longer-isnt-always-a-bad-thing/11279244

Johnston, P. (2019). 'The rise of solo households and how our cities need to adapt'. The Fifth Estate, https://www.thefifthestate.com.au/innovation/residential-2/the-rise-of-solo-households-and-how-our-cities-need-to-adapt/

Karp, P. (2018). ''Epidemic of time theft': Australians work two months' unpaid overtime a year'. *The Guardian*. https://www.theguardian.com/australia-news/2018/nov/21/time-theft-australians-work-two-months-unpaid-overtime-a-year

Marie Claire. (2016). '#BREAKFREE: A Guide On How The World Treats Their Elderly'. *Marie Claire*, https://www.marieclaire.co.uk/life/how-different-countries-treat-the-elderly-20839

Michael Page. (2019). 'The state of work-life balance in Australia'. Michael Page, https://www.michaelpage.com.au/advice/career-advice/work-life-balance/state-work-life-balance-australia

Parents At Work, Karitane, APLEN. (2019). 'National Working Families Report 2019: Executive Summary and Key Findings'. Parents At Work, Karitane, APLEN. http://parentsandcarersatwork.com/wp-content/uploads/2019/10/NWFSurvey-Executive-Summary.pdf

PwC. (2011). 'Millennials at work: Reshaping the workplace'. PwC. https://www.pwc.com/co/es/publicaciones/assets/millennials-at-work.pdf

Redd, L. (2020). 'This Is Elder Abuse: Types, Warning Signs, and How to Report It'. Great Senior Living, https://www.greatseniorliving.com/articles/elder-abuse

The University of Melbourne. 'Life Patterns'. Research Program, The University of Melbourne, https://education.unimelb.edu.au/yrc/research/life-patterns

Tuohy, W. (2019). 'Mia knew 'something had to give' on work-life balance, she's not alone'. *The Sydney Morning Herald*. https://www.smh.com.au/lifestyle/life-and-relationships/is-work-life-balance-dead-and-buried-or-could-help-be-on-the-way-20191213-p53jo2.html

Wood, D. and Griffiths, K. (2019). 'Generation Gap: Ensuring a fair go for younger Australians'. Grattan Institute, https://grattan.edu.au/wp-content/uploads/2019/08/920-Generation-Gap.pdf

Wyn, J. and Cahill, H. (2017). 'A generation dislodged: Why things are tough for Gen Y'. Pursuit, The University of Melbourne, https://pursuit.unimelb.edu.au/articles/a-generation-dislodged-why-things-are-tough-for-gen-y

Wyn, J., Cahill, H., Woodman, D., Cuervo, H., Chesters, J., Cook, J., and Reade, J. (2017). 'Gen Y on Gen Y'. The University of Melbourne, https://findanexpert.unimelb.edu.au/scholarlywork/1277053-gen-y-on-gen-y

Yon, Y., Mikton, C. R., Gassoumis, Z. D., Wilber, K. H. (2017). 'Elder abuse prevalence in community settings: a systematic review and meta-analysis'. The Lancet Global Health, Volume 5, Issue 2, Pages e147-e156, https://www.sciencedirect.com/science/article/pii/S2214109X17300062

Conclusion

Ackerman, C. E. (2020). 'What is Positive Psychology & Why is It Important?' PositivePsychology.com, https://positivepsychology.com/what-is-positive-psychology-definition/

Leonard, J. (2019). 'What is learned helplessness?' Medical News Today, https://www.medicalnewstoday.com/articles/325355

Positive Psychology Training. 'How to Flourish'. Workshop, Positive Psychology Training, http://positivepsychologytraining.co.uk/training/permanent-ways-to-well-being/

Seligman, M. E. P. (2012). *Flourish: A Visionary New Understanding of Happiness and Well-being.* Random House Australia

Seligman, M. E. P. (2018). *The Hope Circuit: A Psychologist's Journey from Helplessness to Optimism.* Penguin Australia

Theodore. (2020). 'PERMA Model of Happiness (Examples + Images)'. Practical Psychology, https://practicalpie.com/perma-model-of-happiness/

Acknowledgements

From David: This book was inspired over many decades by former colleagues and friends who shared their personal stories and took the time to converse with me. These conversations have remained with me, I have reflected on them and I hope those who read this book do too.

Michelle, thank you for enthusiastically explaining why you wanted to be involved. Your effort and insights have made this book possible. Readers – our points of difference are not a falling out; they are something for you to consider. Points of difference are at the centre of democracy, and progress society.

Incredibly, we were able to write this book after only meeting in person once. It demonstrates how business is done in the 2020s. A special mention to Jason, Michelle's husband, whom I have not met, nor spoken with. Jason had many evenings and weekends interrupted by me when I would excitedly call Michelle with an idea!

Nicole, like my first book, this book would not have been possible without your support, understanding and ongoing belief in me. Thank you.

To my children, Anela, Zara and Hugh, this book is for **each of you**. I want the world to be better than the one you have entered.

From Michelle: Firstly, a big thank you to Sylvie and the team at BookPOD for your exceptional service in designing and publishing this book. Thanks also to the Grammar Factory team. It's an honour and a pleasure to work alongside you in the crazy world of publishing.

A huge thank you to my co-author, David, for letting me embark on this journey with you. What an incredible ride it has been. And to think it all started at a last-minute meetup at the Subiaco Hotel! You're the ultimate professional and one of the most passionate people I've ever met. I have loved every minute of working with you.

To all of my friends and extended family, thank you for cheering me on from the sidelines – not just in the process of writing this book, but in general. I am so grateful for all of the love and support.

To my parents, John and Helen, thank you for giving me the confidence and the freedom to pursue all of my dreams – here at home and overseas – no matter how big or small. You instilled in me a lifelong love of reading, history and travel, but also a strong work ethic, which has unequivocally shaped the person I am today. Thanks also to my stepfather, Paul, for all of the help you've given me over the years.

Finally, thank you to my husband, Jase, for being my best friend and my go-to sounding board. I knew when I met you an adventure was going to happen – and I was right. I can't imagine living my life with anyone but you.

About the Authors

David is an author, adjunct professor, advisor, CIO and digital executive. He founded CHANGE lead® in 2019 to enable organisations and their people to realise their full potential. David believes good people have the potential to be great, and that their current knowledge combined with digital fundamentals can reshape entire businesses.

David's international career has spanned multiple industries, much of it involving transformation and the 'next big thing'. He has held a variety of senior roles in companies including John Holland, KPMG, Microsoft, IBM and Capgemini, Prudential UK and CBA.

Since 2015, he has been a member of the Business School Industry Advisory Board and an adjunct professor at Swinburne University of Technology. In 2019, David was invited to chair Swinburne's Course Advisory Committee for the Bachelor of Business Information Technology (BBIT) and Bachelor of Accounting and Business Information Technology (BABIT), formally known as the industry-acknowledged Bachelor of Information Technology (BIT) and Bachelor of Accounting and Information Systems (BAIS).

In 2016, *Computerworld* named David one of its global Premier Technology Leaders. In 2019, he authored *Digital Is Everyone's Business | A Guide to Transition*, which includes testimonials from fourteen CXO leaders. David is also an opinion columnist for *CEOWORLD Magazine*. He lived in London from 2001 to 2010 and is now based in Melbourne, where he lives with his wife and three children.

If you want to learn more about his business and his work, visit www.changelead.com or www.davidbanger.com. If you think David could help your organisation or you, make contact at david@changelead.com.

≈

Michelle is a professional editor, writer, blogger and content strategist. Her passion and goal are one and the same: To help businesses of all shapes and sizes, across Australia and the world, create well-written, meaningful content that sends the right message to the right audience and inspires action.

After beginning her career in journalism, working in print and online, Michelle found her true calling in the field of editing. She has held senior roles in several major companies, including The West Australian Regional Newspaper Group, Private Media and the Australian subsidiary of global publisher The Agora Companies.

From 2017 to 2020, Michelle entered the wonderful world of self-employment, which allowed her to work far and wide, including a stint as a digital nomad in Thailand. Michelle continues to work as a freelance editor for Grammar Factory, which helps entrepreneurs write and publish books in order to build authority and grow their businesses.

Michelle has a double degree in Media and Information (Journalism major) and Communication and Cultural Studies (Theatre Studies major) from Curtin University. *Finding a Better Way* is her first book. She lives in Perth with her family.

If you'd like to get in contact with Michelle, you can email her at michelle@grammarfactory.com. You can also find her on LinkedIn (www.linkedin.com/in/michellestevensonedits) and Instagram (@michstevenson_).

www.ingramcontent.com/pod-product-compliance
Lightning Source LLC
Chambersburg PA
CBHW040142270326
41928CB00023B/3315